To
Woody,
Thank you For
Letting ME fish
Your RIVER.
Thanks
HOMER

Pass the Chicken Please

An Ordinance

Whereas: the frying of chicken is an art and should be considered, and

whereas: the frying of chicken being an art, it is the right of every man, woman and child to enjoy every ecstatic moment in its eating, and

whereas: sinister forces are at work in an attempt to undermine this sacred custom by endorsing the eating of fried chicken with mechanical appliance such as knives, forks and similar other devices, and

whereas: eating fried chicken with the fingers is the very essence of American practicality and provides mankind the only means of completely, logically and properly removing every succulent morsel of the chicken from the bone, and

whereas: the consumption of chicken has increased thousand-fold, and this great increase is multiplying, the gross injustice being foisted on all lovers of fried chicken, and

Whereas: Gainesville is the Poultry Capitol of the World and, therefore, should be leader in preserving this precious American heritage, and

Whereas: someone needs to preserve the inalienable rights of every true American to eat fried chicken with his fingers to his heart's content, be it therefore

Resolved: that the Gainesville-Hall County Chamber of Commerce, in meeting duly assembled, hereby calls on the City Commission of the City of Gainesville to adopt such ordinances as are necessary making it forever and eternally unlawful to eat fried chicken within the environs of the City of Gainesville, Georgia, in any fashion other than with the fingers.

Adopted this 15th day of January, 1961.

Pass the Chicken Please

The Life and Times of Jesse Jewell

Second Edition

Homer Myers

Pass the Chicken Please
The Life and Times of Jesse Jewell
Second Edition 2017

Published by:
Homer's Porch Publishing
P. O. Box 395
Talmo, Georgia 30575

Book and Cover Design by Horton Prather

Contents

A Preface by Gordon Sawyer

The year was 1950: a business friend was talking; *"Jesse was promoting a community project, which wasn't unusual. He hadn't mentioned money yet, but we knew that was coming. The Corps of Engineers was building Buford Dam, and the new lake was going to cover Gainesville's nine-hole golf course. Jesse figured the city could get enough from the Corps to at least buy the land for a new 18-hole course, and we could get it designed by some famous golf course builder. We could sell off lots between the golf course and the lake for enough to finish the golf course and build a Country Club. Gainesvillians needed to go ahead and get the land (and here came the kicker) and you won't have to put up any cash. All you will have to do will be sign a note 'til Gainesville gets the cash. He already had a spot picked out where some farms were available, and here we were in his Lincoln going to see it. He took us all the way out of town, across the Chattahoochee (River) and up a dirt road. We got out and walked a ways and came to an open spot where we could see the bottomland along the river. There, Jesse stops and waves his arms and says: 'Look at that. When the dam is finished, water will cover this whole area up to about right there, and the first fairway will go out that ridge, and the clubhouse will go down there...' He was on a roll, but all I could see was scrub oaks and red clay, and all I could feel was the chiggers chewing on my legs."*

Jesse Jewell could see things others could not see. In the 1930's for a farm to have a few chickens meant egg production.

vii

Farmers bought their favorite baby chicks in the springtime, and they came in boxes delivered by the mailman. They kept the hens for egg production, and sold (or ate) the young roosters as "Spring Fryers." The laying flock ate corn produced on the farm and the eggs (sold on Saturday when the family went to town) provided "Mama's egg money". All across America in the 1930's it was common knowledge there was no way a living could be made from growing and selling frying chickens. Spring fryers were, and always would be, a tasty by-product of egg production.

Jesse Jewell, looking for a better way to make a living, saw something different. Looking from the consumer's side he saw that people liked fried chicken, and he figured it they could get fryers the year 'round they would buy them. Not only that, more people were moving into cities and those super stores were being developed. Hadn't he already been selling fryers in Miami?

The demand for chicken meat grew rapidly in World War II, especially in the military, and Jewell developed a system for producing more chickens the year 'round. It came to be called "vertical integration" and it turned out "pan ready" frying chicken.

As Homer Myers describes in this book the early "broiler business" in Northeast Georgia was lively, often controversial, and ready-made for the sales ability and drive of Jesse Jewell. All were welcome to join in, and a lot of people other than Jesse became a part of this development.

But it seems fair to say it was Jesse Jewell, more than most, who saw that this fledgling industry had the potential for providing chicken meat to housewives all across America. He could see it as a major competitor for beef and pork, and the salesman in his soul led him to carry out that vision. There was a large selling job to be done, and at the end of World War II, he began to tackle it in the American marketplace as well as at home. Jesse Jewell could see this new industry producing "the tastiest, healthiest meat in the world" and it would come from Gainesville, Georgia, "the garden spot of the universe." He was never bashful when talking about his product or his hometown.

At the end of World War II, the older poultry areas—the "egg basket of America" in the Midwest, New England, other areas, expected the new "broiler industry" to wither and return to its "proper place" as a by-product of the egg industry.

When the old Midwest-dominated poultry organizations failed to get excited about the possibilities of the new broiler industry, Jesse was involved in starting   the Southeastern Poultry and Egg Association. He traveled widely, selling this new chicken, hired an advertising agency, and used the newly popular television to reach the customer. He traveled the Eastern United States selling chain stores and meat markets on his products, and enticing food editors to print new recipes using chicken.

He sold his new friends in the broiler industry on the idea of a national advertising campaign for broilers, convincing them that as the market grew, the industry could grow and prosper. That was the start of the National Broiler Council, and Jesse Jewell was its first president. He bought a company airplane and spent both time and money promoting to the marketplace and to the industry itself. His enthusiasm for the opportunities offered by the American free-market system spilled over into the wider business community, and he became president of the Georgia State Chamber of Commerce and a board member of the U.S. Chamber of Commerce. And back home, much to the consternation of some Georgia poultry men, he invited one-and-all, from anywhere, to visit his company and see how J.D. Jewell, Inc. got the job done.

In 1970, as research was being done for the book, The Agribusiness Poultry Industry: A History of Its Development, a survey was sent to a large number of recognized poultry leaders and educators and one line made this request: "Please list the 10 men you feel contributed most to the development of the modern agribusiness poultry industry." More than 200 names were mentioned, representing all phases of the industry and all areas of the country, but only one name totally dominated the returns. That name was Jesse Jewell.

Always enthusiastic, Jesse Jewell had worked hard to lay a foundation for the modern agribusiness poultry industry, and in so doing he had become somewhat of a legend, known and respected all over America.

But what was he like, really? What was it like to live and work with this legend? And who were the people around him who cheered him on, and who operated the company while Jesse built an industry? Homer Myers has interviewed more than 40 people who knew Jesse Jewell personally, and knew the industry he launched.From those interviews, and extensive research, Homer has created this very readable and personal biography of Jesse Jewell. In so doing, Homer has done a great service for the poultry industry and especially those of us who knew, or knew of, Jesse Jewell.

Gordon Sawyer

Gainesville, Georgia

2008

P.S.—There is a point on Gainesville's Robert Trent Jones designed golf course where you can see the cool blue of Lake Lanier beyond long, green fairways. It is a public golf course, open to one and all. Stately homes surround the course, and at the end of the peninsula stands the Chattahoochee Country Club. Across the Chattahoochee River, back in downtown Gainesville, on Jesse Jewell Boulevard, just across from the place where the Jewell office once stood, stands a tall white marble statue with a chicken on top.

Acknowledgements

If ever a book needed a few pages of acknowledgements, this one does. Without the people mentioned here, there is no story. This story is their story. They lived and worked most of their lives during poultry's golden age. Every industry has a golden age, railroads, automobiles, telephones and others in the pages of free market history, and usually, it is in the early years of excitement and uncertainty that we look back and recall those years as times of opportunity and disappointment accompanied with passion. That Jesse Jewell was the Henry Ford of poultry no one disputes, but if he could tell us one thing today ~ it would be that a lot of talented men and women, some associated with him and some competitors, came along during the years that he built his business, and together, they collectively built the industry . The idea of a book about the life of Jesse Jewell originated from artist Ann Brodie Hill, who while helping me with my newsletter, The Porch, suggested that I consider the project. At first, I didn't take the idea seriously, but it would never leave me alone. When I called Jack Prince, the only family member that I knew at the time, I told him that I would not even consider starting without the permission and blessing of the family. Jack, along with Gordon Sawyer, was instrumental in helping to assemble a list of names for interviews. Renee, my wife, came home with a tape recorder and showed me how to use it. As I began to call folks, most of whom I did not know, it was amazing how willing they were to help. Three of those individuals have passed from this life since the interview with them. Ben Carter, who served as comptroller during the company's building years, gave a look inside the company and Jesse's style of management that was invaluable. Joe Hatfield, a legend himself in the industry, helped give me a grasp of the industry's early years in North Georgia and the Southeast. Haskel Stratton, the dedicated and loyal employee whose work ethic was equal to Jesse's, shared how the company survived some years solely from the profits of the offal plant.

Everyone who was interviewed and recorded made their own contribution. Space allows for me only to mention the rest by name in alphabetical order. Some writers can get by with one proofreader; I needed several. Specific thanks to English and literature professor, Wyoma Newman, who combined their efforts to the almost insurmountable task of correcting, and sometimes re-writing my many goofs. The fact that they all maintained their sanity is remarkable.

Lastly, to the Jewell Family, of which I now feel a part of, I can only say THANKS. Pat Prince and I shared moments of tears and laughter together that I will always treasure. Her daughter, Deb Kroll and son-in-law Bob, Renee and I now consider friends. Without Deb's inventory of photographs and memorabilia, the story would be incomplete. The dynamic personality and charm of Jay MacIntosh swept me away as she has done most of the men she has ever met.

Coy Skaggs, an industry leader himself, described his good friend, Jesse Jewell, to be "generous to a fault." My sister, Sidney Wyvonne Estes was the first person to read this book after the folks at Georgia Printing Company and Wyoma Newman. She called me after completing it to offer her compliments and critique. One of her first comments was that it seemed that money, or at least the acquiring and hoarding of it, was not important to Jesse Jewell. The opinion of some of those interviewed was that Jesse was not particularly a "good" business man. That may depend on how one defines "good." But as a visionary and motivator of people, all agree he was without question, the best they ever knew. In all interviews (over sixty) no one else suggesting otherwise. He lived a rich and wonderful life, and my life is richer for having the opportunity to write about his life.

CONTRIBUTORS BY INTERVIEW

Jimmy Bagwell

Barbara Bruce

Ethel Caras

Jan Cooley

Tom Folger, Jr.

Jeannine Payne Fortner

Bob Fowler

Lowell Fulenwider

Nell Fulenwider

Keith & Lida Gorgan

Bob Hamerick

Richard Harris

Skip Hope

Walter & Joan Jackson

John Jacobs

Ed Jared

Diane Magnus

Jack McKibbon

L. P. & Margaret McNeal

Ed Parks

Leonard Parks

Tom Paris

Wilbur Ramsey

George Romberg

Bob Sealey

Lorry Schrage

Tennett Lee Slack

Bob Small

Bill Stowe

W. L. Tatum

Max Ward

Phillip Wilheit

David Wilkins

CHAPTER 1

IT IS AT YOUR DISCRETION MEN ARE MADE GREAT AND
GIVEN STRENGTH—1ST CHRONICLES 29:10 & 11

Edgar H. Jewell Sr.

On a humid Saturday morning in the summer of 1909, nine year old Edgar H. Jewell Jr., inadvertently overheard the conversation of several adult family members gathered in the dining room of the family home. Located approximately three blocks from the center of downtown Gainesville, Georgia, the house was also within walking distance of at least two of the businesses that his very successful father, Edgar Sr., owned. In hushed tones, the gist of the conversation was concerned with the whereabouts of the senior Jewell who had not been "well" lately.

As different ones went searching in the direction of the feed and seed warehouse and the gas light company that his dad owned and operated, Edgar Jr. started to the barn where he and several neighborhood playmates would spend a good portion of their day. As he entered, the early morning sunlight had not yet illuminated the large hall that separated the stables to each side of the conventionally built barn. When his squinted eyes became focused, there, suspended in front of his face, were the feet of his father whose body was hanging from the barn rafters.

Edgar H. Jewell Sr. was raised in the post-Civil War poverty of the South. But as an astute businessman, he had amassed a list of several successful business enterprises by the time he married Tallulah Dickson of Pine Level, Alabama who had come to the campus of Brenau College in 1893 as an art teacher. An all-women's college at the time, Brenau College lent an air of sophistication to the small town of Gainesville from which dirt highways led to smaller

Mary Tallulah 'Dickson' Jewell

towns of Cleveland, Dahlonega, Dawsonville, and other points north in the Blue Ridge Mountains. These north Georgia communities resembled their Appalachian neighbors in western North Carolina and eastern Tennessee more than the post antebellum communities to their south in the piedmont section of Georgia . The demographics of the region with its smaller farms and an independent people with a strong rural work ethic would prove to be crucial to the future of the second surviving son of Edgar Jewell, Sr. who would someday recognize the potential of these farmers and together with their labor and his vision, build an industry.

No one living knows or ever heard discussed how seven year old Jesse Dickson Jewell responded to his father's death. In the days following the funeral, and well into Jesse's adulthood, it was only referred to as an untimely and unfortunate event, not suicide. If such tragedy at an early age can mark a man and limit his potential, then Jesse Jewell was the exception. Although the surviving relatives and friends of the family only recall an uneventful childhood for Jesse, the resilience of his mother Tallulah, and being surrounded by family, made for a normal childhood for a boy who did not show early signs of genius or any distinction other than average . Growing up in town, Jesse's teenage years were spent working at the family feed store and attending Gainesville High School where he recorded slightly higher than average grades. He was well liked and made friends easily.

Jesse (approximately age 10)

Pictured left to right: Furman, Mary, Margaret, Jesse and Ed

Jesse pictured on the left with siblings, Mary (center) and Ed (right)

Gainesville, like the rest of the country was enjoying the prosperity of the decade following the economic panic of 1893. Even though the Deep South was well behind the North East and the rest of the country economically, Gainesville claimed the location as the point of departure for resorts like White Sulphur Springs and vacation spots farther north into the North Georgia and North Carolina mountains. The town also boasted the first street lights south of Baltimore and north of Atlanta. (Jesse's father Edgar had led the consortium that provided the as lights.) A street car route ran through Green Street and later extended all the way to the mill village community of New Holland. The local newspaper, *The Gainesville Eagle* brought national events like the heavyweight championship victory of Jack Johnson and the racial unrest around the country that followed, to the front porches of Gainesville's residents. A vibrant community of retailers occupied the brick fronted two story buildings on all four sides of the square. On Saturday afternoons the streets surrounding the Confederate soldier statue, referred to as Old Joe, were clogged with horse and buggy and mule and wagon traffic. Later, in the 20's these would be replaced by Ford Model A and T cars and trucks, and eventually Chevrolets, since the latter had started competing with Mr. Ford in 1911. As blocks of the city developed south of the square, successful and locally owned manufacturing companies built their facilities along with large brick warehouses for storing hardware, dry goods and building materials. Georgia Chair Company had originally been located in the town of Flowery Branch about fifteen miles south towards Atlanta. When it was destroyed by fire, manager and foreman, Harry Bagwell, moved to Austell, Georgia to a similar position to provide for his young family. The group of investors, who had started the company with the proven Bagwell, lost their enthusiasm for its continuance and sold out to Charles Edmondson. Edmondson bought Georgia Chair counting on enticing Bagwell to return. He successfully brought Harry Bagwell back as manager and eventually as partner. Early on in its existence, Gainesville had attracted a large professional community including attorneys and physicians who served the mountain towns and counties along with the residents of Hall County and its ever expanding county seat. But it was the business owners and entrepreneurs along with their banking friends who were the men, and even some of the women, who shaped the community and determined its growth. One of those women was Jesse's mother, Tallulah, who not only kept the feed business going, but acquired a reputation as an honest but shrewd business owner.

The success of business owners like Edmondson and Bagwell, whose plant was quickly approaching one hundred employees, and the recent start-up of City Ice, another company that would have a significant role in Jesse's future, could not have gone unnoticed by the young man who would also someday shape the future of his hometown and an industry.

Son and grandson of Harry Bagwell, Sr:
Jim Bagwell, president of Georgia Chair,
and Harry Bagwell, vice president

Early days of Georgia Chair, founders and sons. (left to right) Jimmy Bagwell, Harry Bagwell, Austin Edmondson, Charles Edmondson

In his bestselling book, *"An Empire of Wealth,"* John Steele Gordon gives the account of how the U.S. became the world's leading exporter of ice. The industry had been started from the practice of New England residents cutting blocks of ice from the ponds and lakes during the winter months and keeping it in ice cellars throughout the summer. With the invention and use of the steam powered sawmills, tons of sawdust provided the perfect insulator for shipping ice. The lucrative shipping of ice to many parts of the world as far away as British-controlled India was new common business practice. By the turn of the century, ice had become more than an oddity in the homes of middle class America, especially in the towns and cities where the proximity of houses allowed for a profitable delivery route. In 1919, just having graduated from Texas A&M, Carl Romberg I came to Gainesville and started working for Gainesville Ice & Coal. Like most other ice companies, it was necessary to supplant sales during the winter months with coal, which was delivered to the same homes, on the same route, by the same horse and wagons that were used to haul ice to the ice boxes located in the kitchens of their customers. As the "Roaring 20's" roared ahead both culturally and economically, Carl I, who had been joined by his brother Conrad, bought out the investment group in New York and started to build one of the most successful closely held businesses north of Atlanta . In the decade during and following World War II, the ice they produced would be critical to the expansion of the poultry industry.

Carl Romberg (left) and brother Conrad Romberg (middle), founders of City Ice and Food Services Equipment, and Conrad's son Carl Romberg (right)

In the meantime, poultry would remain a sideline farm commodity mostly operated by the farmer's wife. In an extensively researched history of the development of the poultry industry, and his book, *"The Agribusiness Poultry Industry"*, Gordon Sawyer writes, "The old system of poultry raising belonged to the farmer's wife. She counted on the 'egg money' to buy her groceries and her special things when she went to town and sold the eggs. She also provided the labor for taking care of the chickens". In other words, real men grew out hogs and cattle so the feed, fertilizer and seed store operated by Tallulah Jewell only counted on a small part of the sales to come from chicken feed. Although the business had continued to grow under her management, this was still true in 1914 when she married widower Leonard Cranford Loudermilk. The two families merged five children each into a large spacious home some few blocks from where the Jewell-Loudermilk warehouse was located at the corner of Maple Street. Ironically, today a major corridor named Jesse Jewell

7

Parkway, dividing downtown Gainesville's business and government district, covers much of what was the original location. Mr. Loudermilk, who was a devout Christian and was liked and respected by everyone who knew him, brought harmony and consistency to the newly blended household and the business as well.

These were heady days for Gainesville and the communities in the surrounding vicinity. Gordon Sawyer notes that, "the boll weevil swept through Georgia's cotton in 1920 and farmers all over the state began to look for sources of income." But in just a few miles of the square, two large textile mills had been built providing modern housing with paved streets within walking distance of the mills, mill village churches, a mill village school for the employee's children, and the best in athletic fields and educational facilities. These jobs were earnestly sought by families who were raising their children, or had been raised in clapboard shanties on share cropping farms, with their stately outhouses in view from the back door and without running water. In nearby Gainesville, streets lined with sidewalks led to stores and shops, and even to the front of the tallest building south of Charlotte, North Carolina until you arrived in Atlanta. The Jackson Building, completed in 1915, boasted five floors of office space, a marble entryway, an electric elevator, and resembled a scaled down version of the Empire State Building. When county folks left Gainesville to return home after a Saturday afternoon of shopping, or just hanging around the square whittling and trading knives, they could say that they really had "been to town." Far away, the Bolshevik revolution that would eventually enslave all of Eastern in Europe, was festering a civil war and an unknown Italian radical by the name of Mussolini was preaching Fascism. By contrast, in America, home of the free (or at least the white, free) and home to the free market system, life was good. Her boys, or at least some of them, were returning home from the 'Great War' and robber barons were making headlines by making themselves sinfully rich. This was the world a young Jesse Dickson Jewell faced as he left home to enter the Georgia Institute of Technology.

Demetrious Nicolaus Karadmitris was born in a small Greek village where generations of his family had lived, worked, and died for several centuries. His name would change to Jimmy Caras when he reached America where he would establish a lifetime friendship with Jesse Jewell. But long before meeting Jesse, his odyssey would entail traveling through Germany, France and Spain before embarking on a freighter bound for Mexico. He and a young companion had paid their life savings (one hundred and fifty American dollars and all their cigarettes) to secure passage, which also required them to work 16-hour shifts if they wanted to eat during the trip.

Jimmy Caras as a World War I Soldier

Jimmy had been conscripted into the Greek army during World War I as a teenager, but all his previous experiences, including hard work on the farm, did not prepare him for the rigors of living in the hold of a ship for the weeks required to complete the Atlantic crossing. Initial landfall was made in Havana, Cuba. Learning they were in danger of being discovered and deported back to Europe, Jimmy took refuge as a stowaway on another commercial vessel that finally docked in New Orleans. Working his way across several states and eventually up the peninsula of Florida, the young Greek immigrant found work, lodging and support from other Greek families who provided much of the back breaking labor in the docks and commercial ports on the Florida coast. Jimmy's real talent though was cooking and making people happy. His passion for owning a restaurant combined with a God given gift for entrepreneurship would eventually lead to the crossing of paths and a bond of friendship with another yet-to-bloom entrepreneur seven years his junior who was currently struggling with the rigorous curriculum at Georgia Tech .

Initially, Jesse had thought that he wanted to be a civil engineer but the endless succession of calculus and algebra began to give him second thoughts. At the end of two years at Tech, Jesse returned home and announced that he and a friend were headed to the University of Alabama where he would pursue a major in business. Eighty-five years later, most of Jesse Jewell's surviving relatives were too young to recall the details of the Loudermilk-Jewell home life while Jesse pursued higher education. However, it is generally accepted that the home was harmonious among the step-brothers and step-sisters brought together with the marriage of Tallulah Jewell and Leonard Loudermilk. The step-siblings got along well enough, and later as young adults, Joe Loudermilk would wed his step sister Mary Jewell in what was accepted in the community as an "all together proper union" of the two non- blood related siblings. The marriage would result not only in many happy years together, but also in the creation of one of Gainesville's most successful property and casualty insurance agencies. The Jewell-Loudermilk Feed Store was doing well also, but not well enough to provide tuition funds for Jesse. Although no one knows for sure how it came about, sometime during his tenure in Tuscaloosa, Jesse was given the opportunity to work as a surveyor in Florida. The Sunshine State was quickly transforming from a rural Southern farm economy surrounded on both coasts by small fishing villages and vast areas of uninhabited land, to a land of real estate opportunity. The uninhabited coast, both beaches and marsh, were quickly being marketed in a feverish pace that matched the mood and economic boom of the "Roaring Twenties." In 1926, Miami alone boasted 25,000 agents working from 2,000 offices providing the grease that turned the wheels of real estate transactions. In addition to supplying plenty of surveying work for Jesse, the short lived prosperity of the Florida real estate boom provided thousands of unskilled laborers construction jobs, hotel and restaurant employment, and specifically for Jimmy Caras, dishes to wash. It seemed that the entire country was giddy about the potential of becoming rich. If one was not already rich, he didn't have to look far to see a brother-in-law, uncle or former class mate who was already rich (at least on paper) and conclude that it was just a matter of time before his stock portfolio would be measured in six digits or more. President Hoover had even been quoted as proclaiming, "we have conquered poverty in our time." From the ever expanding marketing of illegal booze by gangsters like Al Capone and the demand for "White Lighting" manufactured by the moonshiners of southern Appalachia, openly sold in shot houses throughout the cities of the Bible belt, legal and not-so-legal businesses and industry were expanding exponentially. In one of the best books written about the Great Depression, co-authors Gordon Thomas and Max Morgan Witts give a glimpse of the culture of the 'Roaring' years leading up to the Crash of 29: "In 1929 more people went to movies than to churches or synagogues...Trinity Church stands grand (but with sparse attendance) at the top of Wall Street, a reminder that mammon and God have come to an easy fellowship". Once again history would show that almost without exception, from the "Tulip Bulb" bubble of 15th century Holland to the world wide Great Depression of the thirties, economic calamity is caused by greed, followed by fear and panic. The oversold and inflated land in Florida, often found to be covered by water upon the arrival of its new owners, would begin to lose the "boom" about three years before the "Roar" was being exhaled from the Roaring 20's and Wall Street. In late 1928, the collapse began and accelerated to a crash by the following year. Years later, encouraged to record his memoirs by his children, one can almost hear the strong Greek accent of Jimmy Caras as he writes, "Thez lost it all. Soon the boom start to go down and everybody leave, most loozers...so we leave to Georgia and satisfied we don't go bank rupsi. I come to Macon with $300 and go to work in lunch room."

Jesse left too, for home. No one recalls how he got home, although most likely he used one of the more common modes of transportation of the day; he hitchhiked. No one recalls his arrival back in Gainesville which apparently went unnoticed since so many men, young and old, were already aimlessly traveling the country by foot and rail looking for a day's work and a meal. Although Jesse could not be classified as a true "hobo", there is no doubt about his returning broke and unemployed. It would be less than a year before thousands of men would begin to join him as the ranks of the unemployed began to swell. On the other hand, Jimmy Caras was a rare and fortunate exception. Finding work at Macon's popular Plaza Café, he was last in the pecking order of the four cooks in the kitchen. Two of Jimmy's co-workers who held seniority over him were white and regularly enjoyed making ridicule of his strong accent. Actually, the young and athletically built man, barely spoke any English. But the chief cook and kitchen boss was a black man who would not only teach Jimmy English, but of much greater importance, Southern black cooking.

On December 3rd, 1929 just barely over a month since Black Tuesday, a well- meaning but naive Herbert Hoover assured the U.S. Congress that, "the worst is over." There was no way that he nor anyone else could have known that the recent economic upheaval was just the beginning of a decade that would not only see fortunes of the affluent disappear, but also the family savings, homes and farms of everyday people lost for a generation . Many children of the day would suffer, and some would die, from malnutrition. A dust bowl in the wheat growing plain states would coincide with the economic calamity of the East and cause the greatest migration of people in North America. The tentacles of the Depression would spread to the countries of Europe and particularly to the more industrialized ones sowing the seeds of Socialism and Marxism. The numbers of the American Socialist Party would not see such a rise in membership again until the rise of the intellectual socialism among academia and the elitist of the 90's. Capitalism, without a Judeo- Christian ethic, had broken and left millions destitute, but the Marxist states that would emerge in Eastern Europe and Asia would indeed make everyone equal—equally poor and miserable. The free market system would need the leadership of one of the greatest Socialists who ever lived to help restore

American's quality of life and prosperity. Over the next ten years, it would require The New Deal and World War II to bring good times back, but never back like the extravagances of the 20's. This was the world that young men like Jesse Jewell and Jimmy Caras saw in their rear view mirror, now quickly disappearing. But the future would be coming at them even faster and Jesse and Jimmy would prove, like many of their generation, to be up to the challenge.

For Jesse, the opportunity to prove himself would come quickly. There was nothing really for him to do at the feed store. His mother suggested that he might try to increase the sale of chicken feed to the local farmers. The problem was that the farmers, even in good times, usually did not have the cash to buy feed for their "real" livestock like hogs and cattle, much less for chickens, and these were not good times.

CHAPTER 2

HE WHO FINDS A GOOD WIFE FINDS FAVOR FROM
GOD—SOLOMON

With all the gloom and doom of the last year of the decade and the dismal prospects for the next, both Jesse Jewell and Jimmy Caras would find not just a bright spot, but a bright blinding light that would profoundly impact and greatly influence their futures. Unexpectedly, as most young men later realize, a woman, and not just a woman but a wife—a life mate—would come into each of their lives.

Jimmy Caras as a young aspiring entrepreneur

For Jimmy Caras, the arrival of Ethel came at a time of near disaster and a potentially deadly illness. Jimmy had finally established his own business, a small but successful hot dog and sandwich stand. His customers loved his gregarious personality and his hot dogs. However, with no employees and a work ethic that began to work to his disadvantage, Jimmy almost worked himself to death. The sickness that put him to bed for ninety days was never accurately diagnosed, but it was enough to put the determined, and up until now, healthy young man on his back. A recent high

Jimmy and Ethel Caras successfully operated both the Mayflower and then the Imperial Restaurant, two of Gainesville's prominent restaurants of the time.

school graduate and daughter of Jimmy's friend and mentor, Domingo (Martinez) Martin, a Portuguese immigrant, had been helping part time in the business. As Jimmy grew sicker, Ethel, who was 20 years younger, stayed constantly at his side and helped nurse him back to good health. The week before he left the hospital, Jimmy, still in his heavy Greek lingo, proposed marriage. Even with the accent it was the most romantic words that the young Macon woman, who everyone said looked like a movie star, had ever heard. With the blessings of her parents properly secured, Jimmy and Ethel would start a marriage that would last 43 years until Jimmy's death in 1980. Long after Jimmy had successfully established his business in Gainesville, Georgia, a friend commented to him that he had brought with him the most beautiful woman who had ever lived in Gainesville when he came to town.

But several years before the marriage of Jimmy and Ethel Caras, Jesse Jewell and a friend were taking a casual stroll on the street of the home of Anna Louise Dorough's parents. Anna Lou was home in Gainesville for the Thanksgiving break from her school teaching job in South Carolina. Sitting in a porch swing, she began to notice the pair of young men approaching. Anna Lou knew Jesse's companion but had never met him. Her parents had moved to Gainesville late in her high school years. The stranger seemed to be staring at her with a slight smile suggesting he knew something that was about to affect them both that she had not yet realized. Jesse almost immediately asked her out and she agreed before realizing that she had been "smitten" by his charisma. As the men left, Anna Lou's sister came out to the porch to inquire about the conversation she had overheard and who that "other man was." Anna Lou replied simply, "He's the man I'm going to marry." She would fail to return to her teaching job the next week and the couple would be married the following spring. Two years later, Patricia Ann would be the first of three daughters who would bless the Jewell home. Pat was born without her father's charisma, but she exceeded him and most of her peers with God given intelligence and an early inclination to hard work and high achievement. The serious minded and quiet little girl would spend all of her childhood and a good portion of her adulthood striving to earn her father's approval and love.

Anna Lou as a young woman about the time she and Jesse met.

CHAPTER 3

A TIME TO TEAR DOWN AND A TIME TO MEND, A TIME
FOR WAR AND A TIME FOR PEACE—SOLOMON

O n a hot August Saturday afternoon in 1933, a young man from rural East Hall County would have the experience of seeing his first 'movie picture show' at the Royal Theater on Main Street, Gainesville. After finishing off a 15 cent hamburger and 6 cent cherry coke at the Dixie Hunt drug store soda fountain on the ground floor of the fanciest hotel north of Atlanta, fourteen year old Wilbur Ramsey and his grandfather walked two doors down the street to purchase their tickets for *"Tarzan of the Apes",* the first of several successful films based on the paperback novels by Edgar Rice Borough's popular series of jungle men of Africa who had been raised by gorillas. With his mouth agape with wonder, Wilbur watched with anticipation as a newsreel showing the completion of the Golden Gate Bridge preceded the movie.

The athletic physique of the Olympic gold medalist Johnny Weissmuller, who played Tarzan in most of the earlier films, so impressed the young Ramsey that he made a life-time commitment to maintain a regimented workout routine which he continues today into his nineties. To celebrate the success of his chicken house operation, Wilbur's grandfather had decided to reward his very serious minded grandson with what was considered almost an extravagance during these Depression years by other family and neighbors. Wilbur had distinguished himself from his peers as a young boy by forfeiting play for work and one of his most successful endeavors was the chicken 'house' that he and his grandfather had built from white oak slabs cut from the family farm. His work ethic had also garnered the attention of a man who regularly visited the Ramsey farm driving a Reo truck that was used to haul feed to his farmer customers and crates of "grown out chickens" back to town. Why Jesse Jewell was partial to the Reo brand truck was never known to Wilbur, but what he was more pleased with was the friendship that existed between Mr. Jewell and Wilbur's father. It seemed to Wilbur that this man who had already began to gain the reputation of changing the chicken business, always seemed to look forward to relaxing on their front porch with a glass of sweet tea and talking with his dad.

At age 15, Wilbur had just graduated from Airline High School, one of several schools scattered across rural Hall County. Typical of most families of the day, Mr. Ramsey barely had the means to feed his family, so sending Wilbur to college was almost impossible. When Mr. Jewell asked Wilbur where he would be attending college, he was so surprised that such a smart business man wouldn't already know that most families like his didn't send their sons and daughters to college, that he didn't answer. But Mr. Jewell continued by asking him to find pencil and paper and write down a couple of names. One of those names was the director of admissions at the University of Georgia and the second name was that of the dean of students. Mr. Jewell's instructions were for Wilbur and his grandfather to travel to the campus, some fifty miles away in Athens, and to meet with both officials. Without explaining any of the details of what had already been discussed, Mr. Jewell assured Wilbur that he not only would be admitted but his room and board, along with tuition would be paid for by a job already secured for him. The road from Gainesville to Athens covered several miles of unpaved roads that could become impassable during the winter months.

Adding to the precariousness of the journey was that the only mode of transportation was his grandfather's old pickup. But young Wilbur Ramsey did make it that day, and would graduate four years later with a degree in agriculture. However, Wilbur never joined a fraternity or indulged in the "college experience" because while he was not in class studying, he was working in his dishwashing and cleaning jobs given to him by the Dean, or running his own laundry business.

Years later, as a very successful poultry man, he would try to do the math on the cost of his education and the revenue produced from his on-campus jobs. Somehow the two figures never reconciled and he suspected that another successful poultry man had subsidized his effort. In addition to acquiring his Agriculture degree, he was commissioned as a 2nd Lieutenant in the U.S. Army. Considering the direction of world events, his timing could not have been more strategic.

Fleet of City Ice delivery trucks in the early 40's.

As Wilbur was leaving for Athens in 1935, Conrad Romberg was guiding the family business to leave the coal business and to diversify into the appliance and refrigeration business. While the ice operation continued to be a steady source of revenue, Conrad observed the trend of more homes having electric appliances and the REAs (Rural Electric Associations) were bringing "lights" to the homes and farms of rural America. Vegetable canning, smokehouse and salt preserving of meat were giving way to freezing. Home freezers replaced much of the shelf space of the family pantry, but the Romberg's would build what was to be a first in North Georgia, a commercial freezer. Freezer space for whole or quartered hogs and cattle, along with a winter's supply of vegetables for the family could be economically rented from The City Ice Company. The ornate brick building on the corner of Main Street and what would decades later become Jesse Jewell Parkway, housed the company offices, the ice production room, and the freezer warehouse. Built with 8/10 oak beams, the red brick building would prove to be a refuge for the Rombergs, their employees and their business neighbor across the street on a fateful and disastrous day in the spring of 1936.

Delivery truck as Conrad Romberg diversified the company into the appliance business.

The Romberg Company/Food Service Equipment continues to be successfully run today by George Romberg (right) and his nephews Carl (left) and Chris (middle.)

William Henry Slack started his auto parts business in Gainesville to meet the increasing demand for low cost but quality parts from a legitimate business that would back up its product. The successful business continues today under the direction of his grandson Henry, but at the time the country remained in the grip of the Depression. Many families by now owned some kind of automobile, but finding replacement parts for the family car, or for a business to find truck parts was much more practical and cost efficient than just trading for a newer one.

On the morning of April 6, 1936, one of Bill's employees came rushing into the parts area and yelled for Mr. Bill to come to the front door. Across the street, standing on the steps leading into his office, Bill's business neighbor was calmly but emphatically ordering Bill and his employees to join him and the City Ice staff in the safety of the stoutly built ice plant. The two young entrepreneurs had become close friends over the years often comparing problems and ideas between themselves. Bill had not really given the weather much thought that morning since he usually arrived at the parts store well before daylight. But now, the sky had become twilight dark again with a strange green hue disappearing over the southeastern horizon. Conrad stayed calm as he quickly ushered everyone into the ether smelling ice plant, but the serious look on his face was that of a commander about to lead his troops into combat.

As a roar could be heard coming from a distance the joking remarks had already ceased, but when the lights went out, leaving the two company owners and their employees in total darkness everyone stopped talking. The next few minutes sounded like what some combat veterans of World War I would later compare to an artillery barrage. One of the young girls who worked as a typist began to cry as a veteran co-worker put her arm around her. A seasoned old black gentleman who had originally delivered ice in the mule and wagon days of the ice company began to calmly pray out loud. The prayer seemed to calm the group until his voice was drowned out by the "hundred freight train like sound." Within minutes it was over. Mr. Conrad was the first to push open the heavy sliding oak doors. The office glass front was gone but the building had remained intact. Not the same could be said for most of downtown and many of the outlying homes and buildings. One cotton mill had collapsed adding to the list of hundreds of fatalities. The town truly resembled a city moments after a bombing raid.

Years later, this writer would hear firsthand as a 92 year old Conrad Romberg recalled the tragic day and the events of the following 72 hours. As he looked north towards the downtown square, smoke had already begun to rise from the fires left in the giant tornado's swath. Some would testify later that there had been more than one tornado. To the families of the dead and missing, it didn't really seem to matter. Without speaking or telling anyone where he was going, Conrad started walking slowly towards his home on Forrest Avenue just a couple of blocks north of the square. One of the few remaining landmarks that were recognizable was the Confederate soldier statue, "Old Joe", which now stood guard over broken trees and overturned cars. Conrad instinctively picked up his pace as he began to hear the screams of those trapped in the burning buildings. He was in a dead run when he busted in the front door of his home. There, he thankfully found his young wife and small children huddled in the living room floor. Again without uttering a word and after seeing that they were safe, he returned to the disaster area. He would not see them again for three days.

He and volunteers from as far away as Colombia, South Carolina and Knoxville, Tennessee would work to pull first the injured survivors, and later, the dead from the debris. He did not recall sleeping during the entire time. His last detail was digging graves at the Alta Vista Cemetery before returning home to his family. Just a block away, another local business had been one of the few in town not to be destroyed or severely damaged by the storm. The Jewell-Loudermilk feed warehouse had been protected from the strong winds and flying debris when three train cars had been blown off the nearby railroad tracks to form a triangular wall of protection around the old building. Jesse Jewell would later credit it to the hand of God.

As parts of Gainesville began to fall to Earth as far away as North and South Carolina, and in the farm yard of the Ramsey residence, Wilbur Ramsey knew something "bad had happened in town." Riding with his uncle to see if they could help, state Highway 23 was so clogged with debris the two had to park about five miles from destruction in the community of Rabbit Town. Both men were stunned by what lay before them as they approached downtown. Wilbur, in the not too distant future would spend three and a half years fighting in the Pacific. He would later recall that he never saw a city more devastated until he arrived as part of the lead unit in the initial occupation of Japan. The city of Gainesville would pause to bury and mourn her dead, clean up her streets, and except for the annual memorial services, not look back. The resilience of the small city and surrounding communities amazed state and federal officials. While initial relief had been graciously accepted from both government and the private sector, the vibrant business community along with homemakers and school children, began to move the city forward.

One of the main players was by now a well-known local boy who was doing good, real good. Although he was working 20 hour days, Jesse Jewell had hit on an idea that was beginning to take off. Misses Tallulah had assigned him a corner of the warehouse to market feed to local farmers. The problem was that the farmers didn't have any money to pay for the feed, much less the chickens that Jesse was encouraging them to buy. The feudal system of share cropping in Middle and South Georgia consisted of a relationship between rich large land owners and their (one step above slavery) tenants: poor families, both black and white who barely existed at the poverty level, growing mostly cotton. But in North Georgia, local feed and seed merchants sold to the smaller farmers who mostly owned their own land. Both merchant and farmer had a mutual trust and respect for each other. Credit was extended in the spring and when crops began to "come in" during the late summer and early fall months, the merchant would be paid in full, sometimes leaving enough for the children to have shoes for the winter and, in a good year, enough coffee and cocoa to supply the kitchen pantry.

Following Thanksgiving, lard was the by-product of 'hog killin', an annual ritual which hopefully would fill the salt box with protein for the coming winter. Corn meal had to be ground from the farmers own production and taken to a nearby mill, usually on a stream big enough to supply water power, where the miller kept part of the meal as payment. While most staples for the family could be home grown or even bought in town, there was one thing that was always in short supply—cash.

Jesse recognized that while his farmer customers were not lacking in work ethic or honesty, they were more short on capital than the typical small business person. Consequently, he decided not only to supply the working capital but also to take over as much risk as possible for these people he had come to know, appreciate and trust. The deal he offered was for the farmer to take the baby chicks on what basically amounted to as an assignment. The farm family would grow them out in about twelve weeks on the feed that Jesse also supplied on credit. Since the farmer's wife and older children could provide most of the needed labor (after school and between other chores) the man of the house could work a 'public job' at the cotton mill or anywhere that offered a regular hourly wage. For the first time since before the Civil War, low and middle income families could actually begin to know what it meant to save a little money for a rainy day.

Gordon Sawyer described the arrangement as "the pattern for the business-farmer team which would eventually grow into the agribusiness concept." Regardless of who claimed credit for the idea it "was Jesse who made it a reality." Where the young son of Tallulah Jewell got the money to get started no one can recall. Although Jesse would credit his mother as the person who instilled in him the strong work ethic and integrity he would become known for, it is unlikely she had the extra resources to help him get started. Perhaps it was his willingness to drive all night from Gainesville to the markets in New York or Miami to deliver ice-packed, "New York Dressed Chicken" on his now one ton REO truck. Depending on whose description you choose, the "New York Dressed" term was a chicken that had been dipped in water just hot enough to remove all the feathers, but with the head, feet and entrails intact; and then placed in wooden barrels packed with hopefully enough ice to make the destination of the market. Of course, the entire process started by cutting the chicken's throat which made it a lot more agreeable to the trip.

Jesse had found a family by the name of Gaddis who not only worked, but also lived in the basement of the Jewell-Loudermilk warehouse where the first chicken processing in Gainesville was born. Initially, Jesse ordered his baby chicks from hatcheries located in the Delmar peninsula or the Midwest where some small commercial poultry operations were already in existence. The baby chicks arrived by rail and the mortality rate was surprisingly low. The conductor and other railroad hands would feed and water the chicks until their arrival. Jesse would often times unload the chicks from the rail car and go directly to a farmer's chicken house. Bill Stowe, who grew up in the Gainesville-Hall County area and worked in the poultry business all his life, is certain, and with good evidence, that his father was the first grower that Jesse contracted. Bill and his father were very proud of their first chicken house. Most of the early versions of a chicken house consisted of rectangular shaped sheds made with timber saw milled off the farmer's land. Heated with coal or heating oil, the crudely built structures with tin roofs were a far cry from the modern mega-houses of today, but they sufficed for a time, a time long enough for Jesse to start and pioneer an industry.

W. L. Tatum, of Tatum Farms, did business internationally from his home base in Dawson County.

Bill Stowe, probably the first grower for Jesse Jewell.

The Early Days of Poultry

The Jewell Plant in its heyday

29

Homer Myers

A look inside the Jewell Farms and Plant

CHAPTER 4

DO YOU SEE A MAN SKILLED IN HIS WORK? HE WILL
SERVE BEFORE KINGS – SOLOMON

Ayear after Gainesville's devastating tornado, the city
hardly showed any signs of the original destruction.
Halfway around the globe however, another city of
somewhat larger population was suffering a tragedy that made
Gainesville's deadly storm pale in comparison. However, this
calamity was of human origin and not the work of Mother
Nature. The mayor of Nanking China met the approaching
Imperial Japanese on the out- skirts of the city and officially
surrendered his helpless 500,000 residents to the mercy of the
invaders, hoping for more lenient terms since he offered no
resistance. Over the next two weeks the mayor would come to
know that it was a grave mistake. The Japanese commander
officially accepted the surrender and then gave the order of the
day. All women above the age of 13 were to be raped. Thousands
of young boys and old men were used for live bayonet practice.
On one afternoon well into the occupation, two high ranking
officers who had been drinking sake, made a wager.
Synchronizing their watches, the man who could behead the
most live Chinese males would win the other man's monthly
pay. The severed heads were placed on a fence in the city to be
photographed for the Tokyo newspapers. Suffice it to say, eight
years later during the war criminal trials that would follow,
evidence was not very difficult to find. The same year, Germany

occupied Austria as world leaders in Europe and America insisted on remaining neutral. The U.S. Senate was almost unanimous in its isolationist mentality. Sadly, it would require thousands of young men to sacrifice their lives to stop the tyranny. As Wilbur Ramsey worked and studied around the clock in Athens, Georgia, to finish his degree, he was oblivious to the harsh reality that it would be he and his generation that would be called upon to sacrifice the blood to defeat Hitler because of the prevailing cowardly judgment of his elders. One of those young men that Wilbur was yet to meet until their life paths intersected because of their affiliation with Jesse Jewell, was Ed Jared. As a teenager, Ed had enrolled in a civilian flight school, but it was his heroics in a world war that would place him in the elite fraternity of those pilots who "flew the hump." For many of Wilbur's and Ed's generation, life had been a dull drudgery as they came to adulthood during the Depression. But as the decade came to a close and history's most encompassing war emerged on the horizon, time seemed to begin to pick up the speed of a freight train at a country road railroad crossing.

Events were moving fast for the young Jewell household during those years as well. In 1932, Barbara Glenn followed her older sister Pat as the second born. Both girls were naturally pretty, but neither would consider themselves to be glamorous. What they may have lacked in self-confidence and glamour was packaged in the youngest of the Jewell girls

Janet (3rd from left)
Gainesville High Majorettes

who came into the world wearing a starlet's smile and endowed with a double dose of her father's charisma. Janet Tallulah Jewell was born in 1937 and although she possessed no physical male attributes, the soon-to-become beautiful blond bombshell, was the son her father never had. At work, Jesse had purchased the warehouse and feed business from his mother and other family members. A fact that would remain unknown to most of Jesse's friends and family for years was that his lifetime friend Howard Fuller had invested the proceeds from the sale of his successful service station on Broad Street into the Jewell Company. Howard, the unassuming but steady counterpart to his hard charging friend Jesse, would work in the company as hatchery manager and remain on the Board of Directors

One of the few remaining photos of the Jewell-Loudermilk Warehouse on Maple Street.

until 1959. Jesse was beginning to assemble the parts that would soon, not only make up his company, but also push into motion the modern poultry industry. As the 1930's came to a close, some Americans were beginning to see a glimmer of economic light at the end of what had been ten years in a very dark tunnel, but now a war was demanding all the goods that could be produced. Ration cards became a way of life as shortages of everything from butter to rubber were patiently endured by most of the population as the country united behind the war effort. While these inconveniences were difficult for consumers, they were good for business, specifically the chicken business.

On a cold morning in January of 1940, Jesse was scheduled to meet his friend Conrad Romberg at the Mayflower Restaurant for a sunrise breakfast before their trip to Washington D.C. In a day of slow mail and no fax machines or e-mails, a sit down across the table meeting was the best means for the two business

Howard Fuller, Jesse Jewell's partner and lifetime friend

owners to complete the military contracts they both needed.

When Jesse arrived, Conrad already was seated at a table. While Jimmy Caras greeted his good friend and took his breakfast order, Jesse's more frugal friend Conrad just ordered coffee, having eaten his breakfast before leaving home. Jesse had secured enough gas ration cards to get him and his companion to Washington and back in his Reo truck, but had planned to at least stay in a nice motel on the way up and back. Once again though, his economy-minded companion persuaded him to stop in what Jesse would later refer to as a "low rent flea infested dump of a motel." For years later, Jesse would good naturedly never let his friend forget it. Regardless of the lack of comforts along the way, the trip produced the successful results that both men sought, resulting in the U.S. Army buying nearly all the chicken Jesse could produce for the next five years, and Conrad's ice being packed around each one.

Competition was almost non-existent for the company could claim starting almost at the same time as Jesse's company. Piedmont Poultry was managed by C. L. (Coach) Payne, a local sports hero and former coach at Young Harris College, who had spent the early years of his working life teaching at the small college town in the North Georgia Mountains. Coach Payne had subsidized his meager teaching pay by working as a surveyor as Jesse had years earlier in Florida. The mother of Zell Miller, destined to become governor and later senator from Georgia, often provided lunch in her home for the struggling educator.

Coach Payne as a player at Gainesville High School during a successful state playoff year

In 1940, when he finally returned home to Gainesville, Coach Payne, much to the consternation of his wife, borrowed the money to start the poultry operation with Tom Paris, Sr., who had already proven himself to be a capable

Coach Payne along with Jack McKibbon, Sr., started Piedmont Poultry shortly after Jesse Jewell started his company.

businessman having built a successful wholesale hardware business. The joint effort of Tom Paris, Sr. and Coach Payne would, like Jesse's, sell all the chicken they could produce for the remaining years of the war. Jesse had one decided advantage; he had started much earlier building the network of farmers who trusted him to buy their chickens and sell them more feed on credit as soon as a new flock could be brought out to their farms.

But Jesse had other ideas for their chickens that no one else had ever envisioned. He was not just a dreamer but a visionary, and the idea of frozen chicken had come to Jesse while trying to meet the logistical needs of the army in transporting the highly perishable product across the country. Conrad Romberg's commercial freezer was the logical and most cost efficient means to begin. Although the housewife had not yet warmed up to the idea of a frozen chicken or a package of frozen breast, legs, or gizzards, the military commissaries found it to be exactly what they needed. Although somewhat ahead of his time, Jesse had initiated the modern concept of how most chicken would be retailed in the future.

Coach Payne at a Poultry Convention meeting

As Jesse's company was growing from meeting the demands of the war effort, Ed Jared and Wilbur Ramsey, although miles apart, were taking their first steps directly into the fray. The Army Rangers were not as defined a unit as they would eventually become. But the need

35

for jungle-trained combat troops, specifically smaller units far behind enemy lines operations, became more apparent as the war in the Pacific intensified. Although too early to become overly optimistic, the naval victories at Midway and Leyte Gulf had reversed the roles of the Japanese to defenders and the Americans, along with their British partners, to that of recapturing the occupied islands. The jungles of Panama provided the perfect training ground for Wilbur Ramsey's unit of young volunteers who would become known as the infamous "Bushmasters," General Douglas MacArthur's most admired fighting force. The group was just in its infancy

Wilbur Ramsey, mentored by Jesse Jewell, was a World War II hero and eventual poultry industry leader.

but plans were already being made for Lt. Ramsey and the Bushmasters to go first before all seven of MacArthur's seven major invasions to liberate the Pacific Islands from the Japanese Imperial Army. While Lt. Ramsey was sleeping under mosquito netting in Panama, the young, brash, Ed Jared was training Army Air Corps Cadets to fly. He was a civilian in a civilian operated flying school and became frustrated because he was training rather than headed into the real action. He decided to fly low over the home of his flight commander when he knew he was home for lunch hoping he would be fired and could then join the active Army Air Corps. It so happened, that Ed's house was two doors away. While his plane, upside down, barely brushed over the tree tops surrounding the house, his wife, Celeste rushed out just in time to see the plane close up. She called the school to report that an idiot had just missed the top of their house and gave them the plane number. Obviously, the plan did not work. He was fined $50.00 and was told that General Hap Arnold wants 50,000 pilots trained next year and you're going to help. Ed later ended up in Misamari, India flying

C-46 aircraft from India over Burma, to air bases in China operated by the 14th Air Force. Their mission was to supply 100 octane gasoline and 500 pound bombs. A typical load would be 23, fifty-five gallon drums of 100 octane gasoline. The Himalaya mountain range, tallest on the planet, offered numerous peaks exceeding twenty thousand feet including its best known, Mt. Everest. Ed had become a member of an elite fraternity that for the remainder of his life and recorded war time history would be known as the "Hump" pilots. The trip over the Hump and back was high risk enough to produce a steady list of casualties. Throw in the Japanese fighters who more often than not provided a reception party on the Burma side, and the trip became more precarious. "There would be no graveside ceremony if you went down in the mountains," Ed recalls.

In Pacific Area

Major Wilbur F. Ramsey, son of Mr. and Mrs. W. O. Ramsey of White Sulphur, who entered the army as second lieutenant, infantry, in 1941, after graduation from Georgia university. He was on duty at Camp Croft, S. C., as motor school instructor, until flying to Panama to join a unit enroute to the Pacific area, where he is serving a regimental supply officer. He wears two battle stars on his Asiatic Pacific ribbon and the broze assault arrow head, and has been awarded the Philippine liberation medal and the Silver Star for service on Luzon. His wife, the former Miss Dixie Chester, is now in San Francisco, Calif., employed as auditor in a government office.

Ed later received an award for the Distinguished Flying Cross and the Air Medal.

Lt. Ramsey was a lean and mean airborne qualified trooper by the time the Panama training was completed. Like Ed Jared, he thought he was ready for combat and traveled with anxious anticipation on the troop trip to the Pacific war zone. In a recorded interview, Lieutenant Ramsey stated about his first engagement: "When I first went over there I thought I was ready to kill as many Japs as I could. But during our first battle I was crawling beside a river that I couldn't even see because of the vegetation. I crawled up beside a buddy and was talking to him when I noticed he wasn't moving. When I rolled him over, (at this point Mr. Ramsey paused as tears welled up in his eyes—then continues) his face was gone. My teeth started chattering and I think they chattered for the next three years." In the letter of commendation that was presented with his first Silver Star, his commanding officer wrote, "On 29 May 1941 during a hurried retreat on the Tinfoan River, and in the face of overwhelming enemy opposition, 1st Lt. Ramsey was able to remove and relocate 60 tons of ammunition during only a few hours and save the entire supply. For his gallantry in action in the Wakede-Sarmi area of Dutch New Guinea, he is awarded the Silver Star."

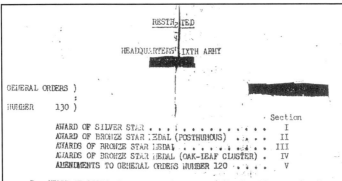

RESTRICTED

HEADQUARTERS SIXTH ARMY

GENERAL ORDERS)
             :
NUMBER   130)

                                                        Section

AWARD OF SILVER STAR   I
AWARD OF BRONZE STAR MEDAL (POSTHUMOUS) II
AWARDS OF BRONZE STAR MEDAL III
AWARDS OF BRONZE STAR MEDAL (OAK-LEAF CLUSTER) . IV
AMENDMENTS TO GENERAL ORDERS NUMBER 120 V

    I. AWARD OF SILVER STAR. By direction of the President, under the provisions of the act of Congress approved 9 July 1918 (Bulletin 43, WD, 1918), a Silver Star is awarded by the Commanding General, Sixth Army, to the following named officer:

    Captain (then First Lieutenant) WILBUR F. RAMSEY, 0415872, Infantry, United States Army. For gallantry in action in the Wakde-Sarmi area, Dutch New Guinea on 29 May 1944. Late in the afternoon an infantry regiment was ordered to withdraw from positions on the left bank of the Tirfoam River. The regimental ammunition dump, containing 80 tons of ammunition, was located on the east bank of the river just inside the existing perimeter. Before transportation could be secured to move the ammunition enemy action forced our troops to withdraw to the back and sides of the dump, leaving the front exposed and unguarded. The entire dump area was by this time extremely vulnerable to enemy sniper, mortar and artillery fire. The enemy was strongly entrenched on the opposite river bank and had excellent observation of our movements. The Regimental Supply Officer gave the order to stand by to destroy the dump. Lieutenant Ramsey, Regimental Munitions Officer, on his own volition organized a party of men and vehicles and with only a few minutes of daylight remaining set out to save the dump. Every available vehicle was pressed into service and work began removing the dump. Many times enemy small arms fire became so intense that the men were forced to cease work and seek cover, resuming their hazardous task under his inspiring leadership. Enemy patrols were operating to the front along the opposite bank of the river, and their activity was rapidly increasing. Darkness was fast approaching and our troops were busily engaged establishing the new defensive perimeter to the east, making the situation at the dump extremely perilous. With superb coolness and determination Lieutenant Ramsey continued to direct the work encouraging the men to still greater efforts, and in spite of all hazards involved the entire dump of eighty tons of ammunition was safely transported to a protected area. Home address: Mrs. Dixie C. Ramsey, (Wife), Gainesville, Georgia.

    II. AWARD OF BRONZE STAR MEDAL (POSTHUMOUS). By direction of the President, under the provisions of Executive Order No. 9419, 4 February 1944 Sect. II, Bulletin 3, WD, 1944), a Bronze Star Medal is awarded posthumously by the Commanding General, Sixth Army, to the following named officer:

RESTRICTED

MacARTHUR VISITS THE BUSHMASTER REUNION IN BALTIMORE

I was delighted to have an invitation to talk to you members of the Bushmaster East Association reunion in Baltimore. It's been a long time since we visited together.

I asked my adjutant to study the battle records of all the divisions and combat teams who fought in the Pacific during World War II. His study was revealing. Here are some things that he found:

The 158th RCT wrote the book of "Jungle Warfare" with its own blood. Any history written about the war in the Pacific would be incomplete if it failed to mention the many military exploits of the Bushmasters. You have set records that will never be broken.

The 158 Infantry Regiment was called to active duty on September 14, 1940 and the regiment was returned to Natl Guard status in 1946- a period of 5 1/2 years on active duty

The 158 RCT was continuously in a combat zone longer than any National Guard unit in all the wars of the U S.

The 158 RCT was the first Army unit to be trained in jungle warfare.

The 158 Infantry Regiment was the first Army unit to be sent overseas after Pearl Harbor.

The 158 Infantry Regiment and the 158 RCT Units traveled farther in their 5 ½ years of active duty than any Army unit in any United States war. From New Orleans, to Panama, to Australia, to New Guinea, to New Britain, to the Philippines, to Japan and then back to the United States.

Now, I'd like to tell you just how you Bushmasters helped the Allies defeat the Japanese in the Southwest Pacific Theater and ultimately help win the war in the Pacific.

The most frustrating time that I experienced in my 55 year military career was when I was ordered by President Franklin D Roosevelt to leave the battle with the Japanese on Bataan and Corregidor and proceed immediately to Australia. A few weeks later, the Philippine government had to surrender, unconditionally, to the Japanese.

On March 15, 1942 my family and I left Corregidor Island and headed for Australia in PT boats where I was ordered to assemble and lead an Allied Army against the Japanese Empire.

After a long and difficult trip through Japanese-controlled waters, my family and I arrived in Australia. At that time, I was informed that most of the Australian Army was in North Africa fighting General Rommel. Later, when I arrived in Brisbane, I learned that there were few Army units left in Australia and that the Australians already decided, that trenches would be dug just north of Brisbane and would be manned by whatever troops were available. When you members of the 158 Infantry Regiment arrived in Brisbane, you were on the frontline without knowing it. If the Japanese had known it, they could have taken over the northern half of Australia without a fight.

In March 1943, you were sent to Port Moresby and again, you were on the frontline. You were there when the Japanese sent a 100 plane raid over Port Moresby. The planes bombed the airstrips around Port Moresby.

You then occupied Milne Bay, Kiriwina Island, Woodlark Island and Goodenough Island waiting for more men, munitions and supplies before launching your first attack.

In February, 1944 you were ordered to attack Arawe, New Britain and advance toward Cape Gloucester with the Marines. Here you faced a determined Japanese Army and you helped drive them out of western New Britain.

After a time for rest and buildup, you were sent to the Sarmi-Wakde area to fight the enemy and to protect the airstrip on Wakde Island. Here again you were on the frontline. After heavy fighting and many casualties, you were replaced by an Army Division. You were then sent to Noemfoor Island to take, hold and protect the airstrips from the enemy. Again you were on the frontline of the fighting against the Japanese.

The 158 RCT left Noemfoor Island on January 1, 1945 to participate in the Lingayen Gulf landing on January 11. Again you were on the frontline of battle with the Japanese in Luzon, Philippines. You fought the hardest battle in your history along the Damortis-Rosario road. You did not retreat in battle; you continued to fight until Company G located and destroyed the 12" gun that was firing against navy ships in the harbor. This heroic effort won Company G a Presidential Unit Citation.

After a brief rest at Tarlac, Luzon, you were sent to Batangas, Luzon, where you had skirmishes with the Japanese troops in the area. After two weeks of sporadic fighting, you were sent to Legaspi, Luzon where you made a landing on Easter Sunday, April 1, 1945. Here again you were on the frontline of fighting against the Japanese stationed in and around Legaspi on the Bicol Peninsula. There you had some hard fighting in the Cituinan Hills. In the months that followed, your unit patrolled along Highway 1 leading to Manila.

After most resistance was gone in the Bicol Peninsula area, you started training for a hostile landing on an island 28 miles south of the island of Kyushu. After the Japanese signed a peace treaty, with almost four years of overseas service completed, with 312 days and nights of the toughest jungle fighting under its belt, the 158 RCT was sent to Utsunomiya, Japan as part of an Army of Occupation. Finally, the 158 RCT was inactivated on January 17, 1946.

Long after the Peace Treaty was signed, World War II was over, and you soldiers were home, a small booklet was published entitled "Top Secret". In it was a description of the secret war plans for the Allies attack of Japan. It stated that more than 40 divisions were scheduled to attack the Japanese homeland. It stated that on D-4, the 158 RCT was scheduled to land on Tanega Shima, a small island off Kyushu. The 40th Division was scheduled to land on a nearby island at the same time; it was to be the first hostile landing on Japanese soil in the last 600 years. You men, based on your great battle record, had been selected to lead in battle, the greatest armada of ships, aircraft and Army units ever assembled in all of the Pacific. We were all thankful that the atom bomb ended the war.

In time, you Bushmasters will be gone, but your military record will live forever!

YOU ARE BRAVE HEROES! YOU ARE AMONG THE BRAVEST OF THE BRAVE! IN EVERY BATTLE, YOU HAVE DEFEATED THE JAPANESE WHO HAD NEVER BEEN DEFEATED IN MODERN HISTORY. I AM PROUD TO SAY- NO GREATER FIGHTING COMBAT TEAM THAN THE 158 RCT HAS EVER DEPLOYED FOR BATTLE.

IT IS MY PLEASURE TO SALUTE YOU, BUSHMASTERS, FOR A JOB WELL DONE AND TO WISH YOU WELL IN YOUR CURRENT ACTIVITIES

Already in his early forties, Jesse Jewell and thousands of other American men were classified as too old for service. Those men and women were depended upon to provide the logistical support to defeat Hitler and Japan. The J.D. Jewell Co. was doing more than its part by not only providing a low cost form of tasty protein to the thousands of troops, but also maintaining the economy by providing jobs at home. Jesse went a step further in what at the time was at best considered controversial. African-Americans had always been relegated to the most difficult and lowest paying jobs in the South. If a black man wanted to work in a factory he would have to move his family to cities like Detroit or Toledo where life was only barely better. Saw milling, working on railroad crews, plowing and such had been his choices since the Civil War. In Gainesville and some other Southern textile towns, a few blacks could be found doing janitorial work in the cotton mills as long as separate restrooms and eating areas were provided.

The J.D. Jewell Co. was one of the first companies in the South to place black workers beside whites on the assembly/processing line. No one knows why Jesse had a heart not only for blacks, but also for poor whites who were struggling to feed their families, but the man who would coin the phrase, "Garden Spot of the World" as he often called Gainesville, refused to turn his attention away from the "poor side of town." In all his impressive list of elected and appointed roles in civic and industry groups that he would hold, one thing that Jesse never lost was his ability to identify with and appreciate the workers who provided the labor for his plants, and the farmers who provided the chickens for the workers to process. By all accounts of those who were closest to him and recall his strengths and weaknesses, Jesse was genuinely generous. His longtime friend, Coy Skaggs said that, "Jesse was generous to a fault." (INSERT BY COY, pg 47) Pat (Jewell) Prince recalls being stopped by a black man while shopping in Gainesville and asked if she was Jesse's daughter. When she confirmed she was, he began to tell her how her father had quietly helped his family during difficult times and had bought the family a television so they could watch a son play college football. Pat also recalls it was not unusual for folks to show up unannounced at the back door of the Jewell's home on Green Street Circle and for her dad to be seen giving them cash. This practice continued throughout the war years and "up until Dad got sick."

But the war years were mercifully coming to a close as well as a chapter of American history. When the war started, the country was basically still an agrarian society with over sixty percent of labor employed on farms and ranches. As the men began to return home, the demand for appliances, cars and their accessories, and a host of other consumer goods provided new opportunity for workers and, just as importantly, start up small businesses. J.D. Jewell Company, on the other hand, was no longer a small business and on 31 December, 1945, in suite 509 of the Jackson Building, in the offices of Wheeler, Robinson and Thurmond, the J.D. Jewell Co. was incorporated. Four days later, Jesse returned with Howard Fuller and the compensation packages were approved, paying Jesse $12,000 annually plus 15% of net profits, Howard Fuller $10,000 annually plus 7 .5% of net profits, and Charles Thurmond (corporate attorney) $4,000 plus 5% of net profits.

As the Jewell Company was being organized, a young attractive Gainesville woman was driving across the United States to meet her returning war hero husband. Dixie Ramsey had had six blissful but brief months with her husband before he had left for war. The couple had not seen each other for over three years. Not far from Fisherman's Wharf, a joyfully sobbing Dixie fell into the arms of a gaunt and battle worn but still strikingly handsome Captain Wilbur Ramsey. After a few days of enjoying a second honeymoon and seeing the sights of the most romantic city in the country, Wilbur started preparing for the drive home. The first thing he had noticed was that the tires on their car were treadless. In his pockets was the three years back pay for combat duty plus an unexpected bonus awarded by the Queen of the Netherlands to those who had helped to liberate her territories.

Although money was not a problem, tire rationing still was. Wilbur entered the tire rationing office in San Francisco wearing the only clothes he owned, his uniform. Knowing how difficult it was to buy tires, he almost apologetically asked the man at the desk if he could buy four tires. As the rationing agent observed Wilbur's uniform he replied, "Young man you don't need four new tires." Before Wilbur could show his disappointment the agent continued, "You need five new tires, one for a spare. Let me know if you need anything else." Looking back Wilbur recalls, "It was a time America appreciated her veterans."

On the long drive home Wilbur had some time to begin to reflect for the first time the historical events he had participated in and witnessed. He had been on a ship next to the Missouri when Japan had made the unconditional surrender to General MacArthur. His unit very likely was the first of the men to enter Japan as part of the occupying force. He had seen the devastation of Hiroshima and Nagasaki. Asked years later if dropping the atomic bomb was necessary, he paused for a moment and replied, "Most likely I wouldn't be here if we hadn't. General MacArthur had conservatively estimated one million casualties to take Japan. Iwo Jima was a recent small example of the cost of military lives to displace the Japs from fortified positions. Multiply that by a thousand and you might get some idea of the cost of taking the main land, not to mention the civilian loss that would have dwarfed Hiroshima and Nagasaki."

Other young men who would become major players in the economy of Gainesville and the poultry industry at large were also returning home. Two of those who came to Gainesville in the years after the war would cross paths with and come to know and admire Jesse Jewell. Max Ward would not arrive in Gainesville until 1950 as an accountant and manager for Allied Mills. His later successes and accomplishments easily place him in the poultry industry's Hall of Fame. Mr. S. H. Grey, who owned Twin Oaks hatchery, recognized the business savvy and potential talent of the young man who held an accounting degree and was a graduate of the Memphis Law School. Max had spent the last year of the war in Guam and Saipan. Mr. Grey saw in Max Ward the opportunity to bring someone in who would provide an avenue for him to sell the business at a pace that would be beneficial to both buyer and seller. Bob Small was still serving as a junior officer on the USS Casablanca as the war came to a close. Although a Georgia Tech graduate, it would be several years before he returned south at the personal invitation of Jesse Jewell who hired him originally as plant engineer.

By the end of January, 1945 the hit song of the year, "A Little Bit on the Lonely Side" had made it to the only record player in the officer's mess at the airfield where Ed Jared's missions originated. Not only was Ed a little bit lonely, but he had seen enough action for a lifetime. As he flew supplies to China, he had distinguished himself as a skilled flyer, he also had been assigned the duty of flying a small plane while searching for downed comrades. His return to the states and eventually Gainesville took a convoluted route that included a position as the Executive Director of the Chamber of Commerce. When Jesse hired Ed away from Charles Smithgalls' radio station WGGA, it was initially to the position of company pilot flying a twin-engine Beechcraft D-18. Later, Ed's contribution in securing military contracts proved to be invaluable to the company. In addition to working as the company pilot, Ed would become sales manager for all military sales.

Insert from Coy Skaggs

Recently I read with interest an article in The Times about Mr. Jesse Jewell.

When my family and I moved to Gainesville in 1954 to run the newly built Pillsbury Feed Mill, I got to know Mr. Jewell very well. Two or three times a week he would come by the feed mill. Talking with him was the highlight of my day. Mr. Jewell was the most unselfish person I have ever known. Space does not permit me to tell all the great things that I learned about Mr. Jewell and his many unselfish acts.

There are three stories I would like to share about Mr. Jewell that show the type of man he was.

First, Mr. Jewell shared with the poultry community and the world his unique knowledge of how to raise, process and market chickens. He kept no secrets and by sharing his knowledge, he saved billions of dollars for the American public by producing quality meat at a very favorable price.

The second story I would like to share demonstrates his generosity. On several visits one year, he mentioned that they were having a good year but they had put a large amount of their chicken inventory into freezers for future delivery; therefore, they were very limited on cash. He worried about not having cash that Christmas to share with his beloved charities. He gave generously to Brenau, University of Georgia, Georgia Tech and goodness knows who else, as well as giving to a number of needy individuals. One morning he walked into the feed mill with a bounce in his step and a big smile on his face. He could hardly wait to tell me how he solved the problem. He had instructed the company treasurer to write these places and tell them that the company was short of cash due to large inventories of frozen chicken, but as they delivered the chickens he would mail them a check for a specific amount. He was so pleased that he had found a way to give to others.

The third story involves a humorous event. We would eat together at the Dixie Hunt Hotel every month or so. I did not think much about it when he told me one day that there was some guy who wanted to cook some chicken for us. This person supposedly had a cooking method that produced "out of this world" tasting chicken. The man turned out to be Col. Harlan Sanders. He wanted Mr. Jewell to back him in what later became Kentucky Fried Chicken. We did not think the chicken was that outstanding and Mr. Jewell did not choose to back him. We laughed at that for years.

Mr. Jewell was a giant of a man.

Coy Skaggs

CHAPTER 5

A GOOD NAME IS MORE IMPORTANT THAN MATERIAL
WEALTH — SOLOMON

As the company was growing exponentially, Jesse came home one day and was surprised, as most parents are, to see that his oldest little girl Pat, had, what seemed like almost overnight, become a young woman. For Howard Fuller, who was witnessing his only child Joan emerge from adolescence to young adulthood, the transformation was more sobering. He and his wife were soon facing an empty nest. The two girls had grown up alternating spending the night in each other's home as best friends while their fathers were building one of the largest poultry businesses in the nation.

Pat never knew why the governor of Georgia had not taken the special-order Hudson with the table and cooler in the back seat, or how her dad had come to own it. She only knew that it provided loads of fun as her mother Anna Lou would drive through the countryside with Mrs. Fuller in the front seat and Pat and Joan in the back playing games on the table and trying to listen to their moms light gossip.

Pat would be an A-student in high school so she did not need the influence of her Chairman of the Trustees father to help her get admitted to Brenau College. Two years later she would be accepted just as easily at University of North Carolina, Chapel Hill, where she would continue her pattern of stellar academic achievement until her graduation.

Her friend Joan was not so academically inclined. Ironically, it seemed that the serious minded Pat should have been Howard's daughter and the charismatic socialite Joan, who approached life as if every day was a party, could have been Jesse's. Joan endured school because it provided a means to an end, that end being spending time with the many friends that she seemed to make as easy as breathing air. She also had her father eating out of the palm of her hand. The normally frugal and practical minded Howard was easily outdone by his only child. Such was the case on the occasion when Joan prevailed on her father to buy her a new red two door coupe after completing her first year at the University of Georgia. Joan had pleaded, pouted and charmed her dad for several days until he finally relented.

Back at UGA the next year, she rewarded his generosity by convincing her childhood boyfriend and her "only true love" Walton Jackson to elope. Walton was a good student and very serious minded much like his soon to be father-in-law. But also like Mr. Fuller, he was no match for Joan's charm. When the marriage was quickly discovered by family and friends, Walton was instructed by his father to go over and have a talk with Mr. Fuller. Walton recalls that as he nervously knocked on the Fullers' front door, he expected he might be punched in the face. To his surprise, a tearful Howard Fuller hugged him and his first words to his new son-in-law were, "I'll be praying for you."

The newlyweds settled into married life back in Athens where Walton would still complete his degree on time but Joan found that she was just "too busy" to finish school. To date the marriage has lasted 54 years.

Not long after the wedding, Jesse would tease his best friend and business partner by asking him how much he had to pay Walton to take Joan off his hands. Unfazed by the teasing, Howard would remain the loyal friend and counter balance to the poultry industry's brightest rising star and pioneer. It wasn't easy. Jesse, according to his good friend Coy Skaggs, had a new idea every day. He once told Coy, who was his regular sounding board that most of his ideas came to him while he was shaving. Many of the ideas would prove to be good; some were not. The one thing that all his ideas had in common, both good and not so good, was that they cost money to implement. Money didn't seem to be important to Jesse. Although he was a sharp dresser and was usually seen in a suit and polished shoes, his only extravagance was a new Lincoln every couple of years.

What was important to Jesse Jewell was people. He took a genuine interest in the lives of employees, customers and friends who in turn appreciated his sincerity. He knew the names of their children and grandchildren and what ball team they played on and how they were doing in school. If their aging parents were sick, he always seemed to know about it and was a prolific note writer. Thank you notes, and more often notes of encouragement were written on note pad paper, business cards, and even napkins.

Coy concluded that the reason money wasn't important to Jesse was that he knew he always had the ability to make more, and make lots of it. However, Coy would say years later that "Jesse Jewell was generous to a fault. He just couldn't turn somebody away who he thought really needed help. Some of those folks took advantage of him."

A classic illustration of Jesse Jewell's inclination to help people make it without expecting or anticipating anything in return was on an occasion that Wilbur Ramsey recalls while he was struggling to get started in the chicken business just a few years after he returned from the war. Wilbur had several businesses going including growing out a house of J.D. Jewell's chickens. When the baby chicks were delivered, many of them were sick and several died. Some mortality among new arrivals was not unusual but Wilbur's flock had higher than normal deaths. However, Wilbur fed and watered the chicks as prescribed by the field man without registering a complaint. Not long after he had taken receipt of his flock, he met Mr. Jewell on the sidewalk in Gainesville. Mr. Jewell stopped and inquired on how his flock was doing. Wilbur replied that things were going well even though he had "lost a few early on." Weeks later, the chicken trucks arrived to catch and haul Wilbur's chickens to the processing plant. Customarily, Wilbur would travel the following day to the Jewell Company offices to pick up his check. After receiving his check for the correct amount, he met Mr. Jewell in the office hallway as he was leaving. Again Mr. Jewell asked him how he had done and at the same time reached and took the check from Wilbur's hand. Without saying anything, he motioned for Wilbur to follow him back in to the payout office. Jesse instructed the clerk to issue a new check and wrote the amount on a note and handed it to the clerk. As he left, he wished Wilbur continued good luck with his next "grow out." When the clerk handed Wilbur the new check, he was shocked to see it was almost double the amount of the first one.

Although yet to be recognized as the most famous name in tho poultry induotry, Jesse Jewell was beginning to gain the reputation of a man anyone could trust. One farmer, who had been growing chickens for Jesse early on, was quoted as saying, "Jesse is like Sears and Roebuck," referring to

Jesse Jewell (2nd from left), Coy Skaggs (far right), and other industry leaders

the large retailer's reputation of the day of 100% customer satisfaction and taking back any purchase that the customer was unhappy with, without question. Looking back with hindsight, many of his business decisions could be valuated as not prudent or wise, but his integrity was never an issue in his business dealings.

The industry, though still in its infancy, was attracting an array of men, including Charles D. Vantress and L. A. "Louie"

Chemell. Gordon Sawyer gives some historical insight into the business lives of both men who were connected by contract but operated separately. Vantress was a graduate of the University of California school of Agriculture and although he would become an industry leader, he was a scientist at heart. Chemell was a salesman who when necessary, could bring his gift of charm and persuasion to a discussion usually always to his advantage. He had managed to acquire the exclusive rights to market the "Vantress male" a genetically unique breed of rooster that had won the coveted "Chicken of Tomorrow" award in 1948 and 1951 at the National Broiler Industry convention. Vantress's famous all white feathered rooster, had become the most sought after breeding male in the industry, but he needed hatchery owners around the country as distributors. Chemell provided those hatcheries throughout several southeastern states but primarily Gainesville, which was the location of his lavish office.

Like any growing industry, poultry listed a who's who of men and women who were for the most part hard working, enterprising and honest. After doing hours of extensive research before completing his book on the history of the industry, Gordon Sawyer writes: "There is no way to name them all, and this is not an attempt to do so. It is an attempt to point out the importance of the period immediately after World War II when a large number of new men entered the broiler industry—not only in Georgia but all across the South. To a large extent, these young men had a good education or got one through the GI Bill; they had seen the world while serving their country; they had experienced responsibility and leadership roles of the very toughest kind; and they were eager to make their own mark in civilian life. The broiler business was a high risk but offered high rewards. These were men (children of the Depression) who felt they had little to lose and much to gain. The men and the industry were made for each other, and the time was right."

Lida Grogan went to work for The J.D. Jewell Company in 1951 as a receptionist. By 1954 she and her husband Keith would make a decision that was increasingly becoming an issue for many young couples at the time. Two income families were not uncommon by then and women in the private and public work place was a phenomena carried over from WWII. The Grogans decided that Lida would stay home with their children. It was a difficult decision, not only would they be giving up the extra income, but Lida loved her job and the people she worked with, and they loved her. Under the tutelage of Kathleen McClure, who not only was office manager but who also had become indispensable to the ever delegating company owner, Lida was trained in several positions. She eventually had held the important task of writing Bills of Lading under the supervision of Furman Greer. In the few years she worked for Jewell, she witnessed the addition of a steady stream of talent and personalities who distinguished the company as one of the most popular places to work in North Georgia. Gordon Sawyer, who was able to have a close-up view from his position at the time as editor of The Poultry Times, writes, "Jewell was one of those people who kept the enthusiasm high. He had a small stand in the lobby of his offices, which would have a new saying on it each day. He would send 'pep talk' booklets to all his people, and to his friends." Sawyer continues, "At one point in the Jewell heyday, someone suggested; 'Take care of the small things, and the big things will take care of themselves.' For several weeks he hammered away at this theme, selling it as avidly as he would sell a load of chickens. It may have been great for the people around him, but it just didn't fit Jesse Jewell. He never was one to spend much time with details, and for this reason as much as any other, probably, he was a master delegator. It took good people and a good organization to be able to delegate effectively. His organization, amid much comment and criticism from many in the industry and out, grew rapidly. He was criticized for squandering the company's money on 'high priced' people and the Jewell creditors were very sensitive to this issue. The people who held to the feed dealer concept insisted a chicken business was a one man operation and all you needed was a good bookkeeper and some field servicemen. Others accused him of trying to imitate 'Big Business.' Although there were periods when the Jewell organization was a highly controversial subject, and a topic of much discussion in the industry, Jewell continued to build his organization his way. He added men like Charles Thurmond, Theron Brown, Hank Conway, George Van Giesen, Charlie Hearn, Edd Pierce and others."

By this time, Jesse's old friend and first employee and partner, was a bit overwhelmed by the arrival of these men who held degrees from well-known schools, and who brought sales, marketing, and management skills to the company . What they did not, or more accurately could not bring was a peer level of accountability to Jesse. To the mild mannered Fuller, who now officially held the title as president but in reality was relegated to the position of hatchery manager, the task of holding his old friend, the boss, in check was becoming much more demanding

J. D. Jewell Company managers in the late 50's.
(left to right) Howard Fuller, Jesse Jewell, Hank Conway,
Charley Thurmond

Officers of Jesse Jewell, Inc.
(left to right) Howard Fuller, Charley Thurmond, George
Van Geisen, Jesse Jewell, Hank Conway, Otis Cato

CHAPTER 6

WHO HAS WOE? WHO HAS SORROW?
HE WHO LINGERS OVER WINE — SOLOMON

J esse Jewell was already well known in the industry by now, holding one after another elected positions of industry organizations . He filled a term as the president of the Georgia Chamber of Commerce. Brenau College continually depended upon his influence in the business and professional community to annually raise funds for the private institution and continually kept him in the position as chairman of the trustees. He was a leader in his church and insisted that his managers follow his example to become involved with and to give back to the community. But Jesse, like all men, had feet of clay. Those who knew him best, and loved him the most, agree without hesitation that he was a functioning alcoholic. Pat Prince recalls her father as a person who could spell bound a room just by his entrance.

Pat Prince today

At local restaurants, people would stop talking and turn to notice when he entered. A weekly family tradition was eating at the Mayflower with Jesse's friend Jimmy Caras on Sunday night. He was so well liked that the family could not get through the meal as friends would come over to their table to stop and chat. For all the things that Pat admired about her father, his drinking habits concerned and scared her. He never once was abusive to her, her younger sisters, or her mother, and even though she didn't want to admit it to herself, he was even more charming and funny when he was drinking, and, he increasingly drank a lot.

Since Gainesville-Hall County was "dry," Jesse had one of his favorite truck drivers to bring back cases of 'Jack Daniels' from trips to Tennessee. Most of his drinking took place in the evenings after work but as time went by, Jesse would get and stay drunk for two weeks at a time. The only person Anna Lou trusted and could turn to was Howard Fuller. For one good reason, Howard was the only person Jesse would listen to when his demon had the best of him. Howard would typically arrive at the Jewell home shortly after Anna Lou called. Howard was shorter than Jesse by several inches, but without any physical contact and with a quiet but commanding voice, he would order Jesse into his car. A 'hospital' in the Atlanta area would be their destination where Howard would leave his friend until he 'dried out.' Afterwards, the ever loyal Howard would return to pick Jesse up. Jesse's one or two week's absence from the office would be explained as an impromptu vacation or sudden business out of town.

The ancient Chattahoochee River had flowed down from the mountains of North Georgia and into the Gulf of Mexico for thousands of years, and past the city of Atlanta for hundreds. In 1946, the U.S. Congress authorized the construction of a dam on the Hall and Gwinnett County lines that would create one of the largest man-made lakes in the world. By 1956, Buford Dam would have backed up the river to the level that the Army Corps of Engineers had designed which placed 38,000 acres of former farmland and the rural communities of five counties under water. While millions of dollars had been spent purchasing the land for a going price of $25 per acre, the funds to clear it of all the houses, barns and pasture fencing were limited resulting in many structures left to be entombed in the depths of the deep water lake . A number of chicken houses that Jesse Jewell's growers had used were covered along with portions of major highways and service stations. The primary intent of the lake was to provide water power for the mega generators at Buford Dam which in turn would eventually supply most of Northeast Georgia, including Atlanta, with electricity. Only a few with a vision for the potential of real estate savvy saw the potential for recreation and development. Years later, land that had originally been bought for $25 per acre would sell for $25,000 per square foot on much of the 692 miles of shore line that surrounded Lake Lanier. What had been a typical part of the South in culture and demographics, Gainesville/Hall County and the surrounding communities now competed with the likes of resorts found in some of the more exclusive enclaves of the country. The resulting prosperity that came to the region could be contributed to by two main factors; the first one obviously being Lake Lanier, the second one was chickens.

White feathered chickens, that had now replaced hogs and cattle on the area farms, were hauled daily to the processing plants on the industrial side of Gainesville. No one seemed to object to the white feathers that were generously sprinkled on the roads and streets of the area because they represented jobs and consistent income. As the first grandchild to Jesse and Anna Lou, Debby Prince and her younger brother Jesse Prince, would regularly be picked up by their now famous grandfather on Sunday mornings and ride with him as he checked on the hatchery and processing plant. Grandfather Jesse would then return them home in time for them to make Sunday school with their parents. On one such trip, Debby remembers complaining to her grandpa that the hatchery "smelled bad." "Oh no, honey," her grandpa replied, "Smells like money to me."

Chickens had come to smell like money to many other business folks as well. The ancillary businesses that began because of what Jesse had started twenty years earlier are numerous. If the poultry industry should ever give an award for

59

the industry's all-time greatest salesman, although the competition would be keen, the likely winner would be Julian Lowell Fulenwider. "Pug" Fulenwider came to Gainesville in the late 40's at the invitation of Louie Chemell to run a feed store in which Chemell had majority interest. It was apparent early on that the two men did not share the same business philosophy and Mr. Pug left to

(left to right) Julian Lowell (Pug) Fulenwider, founder of Chick Supply Company, D.J. Johnson, Lowell Fulenwider and C.L. Jones.

start Blue Ridge Feed with several local investors. As his reputation for utmost integrity and dependability grew, coupled with his quiet and unassuming sales manner, the business prospered. In 1953, he saw the need for a local source of vaccines and medications for the growing number of farmers and producers of chickens. It wasn't difficult for a man of Pug Fulenwider's reputation to convince his silent partners to start "Chick Supply." He would eventually buy the investors out on good terms and the business continues today under third generation management.

(left to right) Lowell Fulenwider, Mark Satterfield, Kenny Mooney, Jay Fulenwider, Mrs. Fulenwider and granddaughter Hannah Fulenwider.

One of Mr. Pug's peers of the time had a bit more difficulty in getting started but would still place himself and his family business in the category of one of the area's best success stories. Tom Wilheit had basically gone bankrupt trying to make a success of a chicken manure processing operation in Pendergrass, Georgia just a few miles south of Gainesville. The process involved heating the raw product to a high temperature resulting in a stench that permeated the surrounding

Tom Wilheit

community. Not only did the locals complain, (justifiably, his son Phillip would laughingly recall) but some of the displeased neighbors started stealing his chickens at night. Either way, it seemed that the business was doomed and the Clemson University graduate was smart enough to know when to cease operation.

Having spent all his life savings on the venture, Tom took a sales job with Patterson Parcel and Paper Company and was given a Studebaker sedan to cover his routes in states from Mississippi to Georgia. Seven year old Phillip remembers seeing his dad only on weekends as he would always be leaving early on Monday morning in the Studebaker. One of his customers was Mr. Paul Delaney with International Paper Company. Together they developed what would become one of the major innovations of the meat packaging business and specifically poultry packaging. "Giblet Wrap" was the impetus for Tom Wilheit to start Wilheit Packaging. The company's only asset was a wooden desk that son Phillip keeps today in the boardroom of the office building adjacent to their huge warehouse just outside of Gainesville.

Phillip Wilheit, now company president, manages the one hundred plus employees that manufacture and distribute products all across the United States. The younger Wilheit, however, has not always enjoyed the reputation of a choir boy. According to Phillip, his father recognized the need for some early on discipline in his son's life and put him to work each summer as soon as school was out doing the most physically

The Wilheit family in Los Angeles for National Convention

demanding and dirtiest jobs the company offered. When Phillip finally graduated from college, he thought he might take some time off to "find himself." What he found instead was that he was to be at work in the warehouse at promptly 5:30 the next morning unless he chose to find himself on his own financial support.

Again, the number of businesses and individuals who came along during the poultry's glory days, which basically coincided with Jesse Jewell's tenure, are too numerous to mention. Lloyd Strickland built the largest hatchery operation in the Southeast in nearby Chestnut Mountain community.

A book has been written about the startup and building of Fieldale Farms, which today is one of the largest poultry companies in the world while the company remains family owned and managed. Although Tom Arrendale has passed away, his partner Joe Hatfield can be found most every day in his office at the Baldwin, Georgia corporate headquarters. During several interviews with Mr. Hatfield, he recalled with precision the events and people who came along at the same time he and partner Tom Arrendale were starting their company. Although he did not have a lot of direct dealing with Jesse Jewell, Mr. Hatfield recalls that Jesse was the kind of fellow that "you didn't have to have a signed contract with, his word was good enough."

The Jewell Company was also the breeding ground for several individuals who left and started successful operations of their own. Bob Sealey would start his own retailing business and would be followed by men like Thereon Brown. Both would find success after their Jewell Company days.

One of the most successful people who left the company to start his own business was Jesse's own son-in-law. While Pat Jewell was completing her education at UNC Chapel Hill, she met and fell in love with a tall slim young paratrooper just out of the service. Jack Prince was born with a radio voice and since radio was the primary medium of the day, he had chosen broadcasting major. Pat invited him down to meet the family and luck was on his side as he hitch hiked a ride from Chapel Hill, N.C. to the front entrance of the Mayflower Restaurant on Main St., Gainesville. When Jack asked for directions to the Jewell home, a man with a heavy Greek accent asked him in turn what his business was with the Jewell family. Upon learning that Jack was courting Pat, Jimmy Caras' suspicious demeanor changed to greeting him as if he were already family. Jimmy insisted on carrying Jack to the front door of his best friend's house.

After Jack finished Chapel Hill, he would work with J.D. Jewell Company until he ran for U.S. Congress. Unfortunately

Jesse holding grandson Jesse Prince with Debbie in background

for Jack, even though by many considered to be the best man for the job, he ran as a Republican. He was ahead of his time politically, since the Democratic "Solid South" had yet to become solidly Republican. Jack would return to the private sector to start a de-boning machine company that his son Jesse Prince continues today.

J. D. Jewell Company managers in the late 50's.
(left to right) Howard Fuller, Jesse Jewell, Hank Conway,
Charley Thurmond.

Jewell Company employees celebrate at a Christmas Party. (1st row floor l-r)
Robert Sealey, Howard Fuller, Charley Thurmond, Lewis Parten. (2nd row
floor l-r) Betty Lathem, Jesse Jewell, Charlsey McConnell, Bobby Hardy, Peggy
Halman, Louise Griffin. (next row sitting l-r) Hank Conway, Theron Brown,
Frances Goforth, Rachel Skelton, Mollie McCrackin. (next 2 rows l-r) Bob
Roper, unidentified, Winfred Vickers, Roy Parks, Haskell Straton, Edd Pierce,
George Green, Clyde Grindle, Clyde Peck, George Van Geisen. (standing by
tree) Mr. Heath. (sitting on right of picture) Sybil Thompson, Lida V. Grogan,
unidentified, Charlie Hearn.

CHAPTER 7

THERE IS AN APPOINTED TIME FOR EVERYTHING
— SOLOMON

In addition to being the decade of the most births in American history, the 50's were ushered in by "I Love Lucy", "The Jack Benny Show" and a host of television shows on the growing number of screens now found in American living rooms . The country's appetite for new appliances had enticed large retailers like Sears to enter the market. Recognizing that his smaller company could not compete with the buying power of the large chain stores, Conrad Romberg steered the family business more towards the restaurant and industrial equipment business where he could compete with the nationwide companies by supplying local service and attention. The poultry business was changing too, and while Jesse and his management team strived to stay ahead, Jesse had some family matters that would require his immediate attention.

Barbara Glenn Jewell was as pretty and almost as smart as her big sister Patricia. Following her to Chapel Hill, it was Barbara's plan to graduate, just as her sister Pat had done, and find a job teaching. As winter semester passed into spring, Barbara had begun to notice some stiffness and soreness in her legs and hips as she walked to class each day. She dismissed it as just fatigue and being out of shape, until her writing became impaired by the same stiffness in her wrist and knuckles. One morning in late spring as the North Carolina climate had begun to soften into milder temperatures; Barbara painfully eased her body out of bed and struggled to walk. After calling Pat who took her to breakfast, her big sister insisted on calling their dad. Over the course of the next few months and numbers of visits to doctors and specialists, Barbara was diagnosed with an onset of acute rheumatoid arthritis. As a specialist explained the condition to Jesse and a tearful Anna Lou, the father who had a difficult time of verbally expressing his unconditional love for his daughters, instantly decided to move Barbara to the hottest and driest climate available in the continental United States, Arizona. Like many of Jesse's peers of his generation, he found hugging and showing affection to his girls to be at best awkward. But so characteristic of Jesse, he immediately began to formulate a solution for Barbara's plight. Business was good, and even had it not been, Jesse would have done whatever was necessary to get Barbara there. After buying a house for her to live in, he helped her to get enrolled in the University of Arizona where she would not only complete her degree but also successfully obtain several advanced degrees. The frequent trips to visit Barbara became a regular part of the Jewells' lives to the extent that Jesse kept a set of golf clubs at her house and eventually bought a condo for him and Anna Lou after Barbara was married. For a while, Barbara would thrive in the Southwest where her happy marriage would produce a daughter, Anna Beth, which greatly pleased her grandmother.

Back in Gainesville, at the April 15 Board of Directors meeting, a motion was made and unanimously approved to purchase life insurance on Jesse and the other key players in the company. It was determined that while the company should acquire $65,000 on Jesse, Howard Fuller would be covered

Telegram approving the life insurance

for$75,000. No explanation was given as to why the company needed $10,000 more on Howard and one can only speculate that some prior coverage was already in place on the majority stock holder. In either case, in a day when $500 and $1000 policies were considered to be the norm, the amounts on Jesse and Howard were huge and probably made for a very successful year for some unknown agent.

Jimmy Caras had started opening the Mayflower at 6:00 a.m. from the first day that he and Ethel had bought the restaurant from the original absentee owner. A loyal stream of customers including blue collar workers, business owners and some professionals had made breakfast at the Mayflower, or at least a cup of coffee, a regular part of their daily routine. Jimmy's ever present smile and good humor, the good food, and the always attractive Ethel made the morning experience at the Mayflower a pleasant way to start the day for the town's early to work crowd, along with some ancient members of the informal but exclusive coffee groups.

On this particular morning, some of the early patrons were reading the paper that "Covered Dixie like the Dew." Below the headlines of the Atlanta Constitution, there was finally some good news from Korea. Under the command of Lt. General Matthew Ridgeway, energized U.S. forces had driven the "People's Army" back across the 38th Parallel. Although the people of North Korea would live in a state of darkness and Marxist oppression for future decades, at the cost of 33,000 lives of America's young men, South Korea's population would remain free to become a major player on the world's economic stage and an example of democracy. Sadly, two decades later, this example of stopping communism would not be repeated in a small neighboring country called Vietnam.

The front page also ran an article, with a follow up piece in the sports section, on the rise of the new Heavy Weight champion. Rocky Marciano was the first white man, following a long succession of black champions, to hold the crown. He would also be the last white champion for a long time as well.

But in this same issue of the morning paper, African-Americans could find a champion in their corner on the opinion and editorial pages. A gifted and nationally known columnist by the name of Ralph McGill continually pricked the conscience of his readers by dispelling the myth that "separate but equal" was, in reality, truly equal.

But on this morning, as Patti Page sang "The Tennessee Waltz" on the juke box, most of the diners at the Mayflower would not give much time to the news from a faraway war in Asia or the idealistic beseeching of Ralph McGill; there were places to go and reasons to rush off to more important things. That was true for everyone except for the three well-dressed strangers who had found a table next to the window facing Main Street. They didn't seem to be in any hurry to order breakfast as they sat contentedly drinking coffee and watching the busy breakfast crowd come and leave with takeout orders. Jimmy Carras had developed a keen sense of perception from his years of surviving his immigration to America and his struggle to succeed in the restaurant business. Rather than have his young waitress continue to serve the dark suited customers, Jimmy took the tray of glasses of ice water along with three breakfast menus and greeted the men at the table cordially. Maybe it was because they did not return the greeting, or maybe it was the prevailing air of smugness he sensed, but Jimmy was just a little weary of his guests.

Finally, one of the men looked up as Ethel made her way across the dining room to deliver menus to some new arrivals and made a comment something to the effect that there were some good looking women in the South. Jimmy replied, "Yea, she's my wife." It may have been Jimmy's heavy Greek accent, or maybe it was the soberness of his demeanor, but the sneer on the man's face was replaced by a look of bewilderment as Jimmy continued, "And they are serving breakfast over at the Dixie Hunt where I think you fellows might be a bit more welcomed." Their mouths fell open as Jimmy retrieved the menus, but no one had to look long at the expression on the face of Jimmy

Carras to get the message that he meant what he said. There wasn't anything to clean from the unused table after the men left, but Jimmy noticed what appeared to be a business card that had been left on the floor under one of the chairs. Jimmy had Ethel confirm what the card said since he was still learning to read as well as speak his second language. As Ethel read, *"Representative: The Amalgamated Meat Cutters and Butcher Workmen of North America,"* Jimmy was already on his way to the small office in the back of the restaurant to call his friend Jesse Jewell.

Some employers are frightened when a labor union starts knocking on the door to their employees, while some get mad and threaten to close down. Jesse Jewell was neither frightened nor mad, but his feelings were hurt. It wasn't that he was naïve or sentimental, but Jesse almost knew each employee's name and something about his or her family. Additionally, he paid more than any other poultry processor, of which there were now several competitors. Even more perplexing to Jesse was how his company had managed to show up on the union's radar screen.

It could have been the high profile industry groups that he had been elected to preside over, or perhaps it was the article in Collier's that had brought the attention of labor. The 15 cents per copy magazine had national circulation and the color pictures of Jesse and other employees had made for good public relations at the time. Still, there was a handful of employees who the organizers were able to convince they were disgruntled and underpaid.

After the adjournment of an evening meeting attended by Jesse, other company managers and representatives of the Union, a disturbance erupted outside the plant as everyone was leaving. Later in congressional hearings, witnesses for the Union would claim that Executive V.P. George Van Giesen threw the first punch. Although the "loyal to the core" Van Giesen denied starting the ruckus, he did not deny decking the union rep. The Amalgamated Meat cutters would never represent more than ten percent of the employees of J.D. Jewell

Co. Inc., yet each year they were given, at Jesse's insistence, the same Christmas bonus that everyone else received.

The trajectory of the poultry industry could now be compared with the rockets that the United States was beginning to send into space to compete with the Russians. It seemed that more competitors were emerging daily. This new competition only encouraged Jesse's continual offering of new ideas that, more often than not, left his Board of Directors and management team wondering about his next brilliant idea. And, perhaps more importantly, how it would be financed. At the 12 January, 1951, Board meeting, a decision was made that would not only change the Jewell Company, but the entire industry as well.

Money was tight and because it was becoming more difficult to acquire more bank loans without drawn out negotiation, the company had been forced to borrow large sums from the life insurance policies on Jesse and other key people. The two million pound capacity freezer was near completion and a nine story feed mill was beyond the planning stage. Jesse Jewell was well ahead of his time but low on cash. Still, he was forever seeing the potential for chicken that no one else had ever envisioned.

Chicken sticks and commercially prepared chicken pot pie were just a few of the ideas he wanted to launch. Comptroller Hank Conway was the bearer of the bad news that the company was spending $3,000 a month on storage space and another $3,000 on interest. Still Jesse was optimistic. The freezer would soon be completed and it would be the first of its kind in the country. Some of the more conservative in attendance including

Jesse's idea to introduce frozen chicken pot pie to the consumer was a little ahead of its time.

his best friend Howard Fuller reminded him that the company still had to stay current with their creditors and suppliers. This was equally important to Jesse who prided himself in being a businessman who not only paid his bills but paid them on time. However, Jesse had always been able to make more money and to him these times were no different than those years of the late 30's and 40's when he could "fly by the seat of his pants." But times were not the same and competitors like Max Ward and others had entered the game. While these men were honest and forthright as Jesse was, they brought a savvy and astute business practice to an industry that had been launched by mavericks like Jesse Jewell. As the January meeting came to a close, and, "following much discussion," a motion was made and "unanimously resolved that as soon as the freezer is complete and in operation, the Company will discontinue selling ice-packed poultry and confine its entire operation to frozen poultry." The Jewell Company and the poultry industry would never be the same.

Herman Talmadge (right), shares a piece of the Jewell Company Chicken with Jesse (left) and an unidentified industry official.

Barbara Glenn Jewell, who was by now well settled and much healthier living in Tucson, Arizona, would soon meet and marry Richard Asmussen also of Tucson. Pat's husband Jack Prince, was performing very well as sales manager, proving that he had the job not just because he was married to the owner's daughter. Plus, Jack and Pat's union had produced a granddaughter, Debby, and within the next four years Jesse and Rebecca Prince would be added to the Jewell family album. One daughter remained at home and she was proving to be more than enough to keep Jesse and Anna Lou from worrying about experiencing an empty nest, and perhaps secretly wishing for it at times. Janet Tallulah Jewel was not only pretty, just like her older sisters, she willed herself to be glamorous. Tall for the times, the long legged blond did look like a model in her Gainesville High majorette uniform. Not only was she the prettiest girl in the school, she, like her sisters, was well above average intelligence. But Janet exhibited an attribute that neither of her sisters ever had-audacity. Along with a generous measure of self-confidence and natural leadership abilities, she was described by underclassman Austin Edmondson as, "the girl who ran the school." She was also very spoiled by her father, she knew it and relished it. Janet turned 16 in 1953, the year before American Bandstand had debuted on television. Times were changing, and for better or worse, so were America's teenagers. The successful and self-assured Janet found that even she was not immune to peer-pressure. She started smoking so she could be accepted by the daughters of some of the most affluent families in town. The clique was small, but the girls in the group were popular and pretty and Janet would become one of them regardless of the cost. Her father knew almost immediately that she had started smoking. During this same year, he would meet with bankers and creditors in long and intense sessions emerging with the go ahead and funds to keep his company on the cutting edge of ingenuity. Negotiating with Janet was proving to be much more difficult than with his bankers or board of directors. Finally a deal was struck. Janet could have her pick of any new car of her choosing as long as she would give up cigarettes. When she drove the white convertible Crown Victoria home for the first time, she actually intended on dropping her smoking habit. When she had started smoking, she had to force herself to enjoy inhaling the smoke that burned her throat and sometimes actually made her nauseated. But by now she was addicted, and even her strong will could not pull her away from the grip of nicotine. Not until her children would come into the world some years later would she be able to leave cigarettes out of her life.

As J.D. Jewell Company was finding it necessary to adapt to the ever changing poultry industry, other local business owners within blocks of the Jewell offices were taking the necessary steps to stay relevant in their respective markets. Georgia Chair was marketing its simple but by now very successful line of oak products internationally. Conrad Romberg had stirred his company to stick with restaurant equipment and retail ice, and avoided selling on credit and becoming more of a finance company than a wholesaler/retailer.

Larger firms were now noticing the increasing poultry activity in North Georgia and specifically Gainesville. Pillsbury decided to send their most promising and proven manager to Gainesville to run their feed mill which they had leased from Jesse Jewell. Coy Skaggs had wrestled with the decision to leave his native Kentucky and come south or to stay in the vicinity of family. When he approached an old friend and associate for advice, the older man said, "Coy, you can stay here close to your family and in-laws and probably at best wear your welcome out in their homes or they will wear out their welcome in yours. And there is a good chance you will be mad at some of them or them mad at you. Take your young wife and family to Gainesville and when you visit on Thanksgiving and Christmas, or any other time, they will be overjoyed to see you and likewise you will be glad to see them."

Coy took the advice and arrived at the front door of the Dixie Hunt Hotel, in February 1954. Housing was in demand so Naomi set up housekeeping in the areas nicest hotel until a home could be found. Charles Thurmond, vice president of the

Jewell Company, would help Coy and Naomi find a home. Coy had met "Mr. Jewell" at an industry function some time earlier and had been impressed, as most people were with the sharp dressed, acclaimed industry leader. Little did he know that his transfer to Gainesville would lead not only to a successful career there, but also a lifetime close friendship with the "Pioneer of the Poultry Industry."

Momma Loudermilk made lunch every day for friends and family who might drop by. Although Jesse was not as regular because of the increasing demands on his schedule, on the days that he could get away he would join other family and who ever might show up. Nephew Leonard Parks always looked forward to Uncle Jesse's attendance. He was funny and usually had candy or other surprises for the kids who happened to be around. Leonard, who would become a U .S .Navy submarine commander years later, had the opportunity to caddy for his famous uncle. He remembers Jesse as being just an average golfer but he never witnessed Uncle Jesse losing his temper or becoming frustrated while playing. Jesse loved the game which had to be one of the motivations for initiating the Chattahoochee Country Club.

As it filled to full capacity, Lake Lanier had covered the only course in town. Gordon Sawyer recalls receiving an unexpected visit from Mr. Jewell in his office one morning. Jesse was approaching local business and professional folks to invest $1000 in the soon-to-be-built club that would be adjacent to the city's municipal course. When Jesse left he had a check from Gordon that represented a large investment at the time, especially for a young man with a growing family. But Gordon found it difficult, as most did, to say no to Jesse Jewell. Years later he came to appreciate Mr. Jewell's inclusion of him in the endeavor.

Coy Skaggs attributes one of Jesse Jewell's lesser recognized contributions to the industry that has been overshadowed by some of his better known innovations like Vertical Integration. Gordon Sawyer defines "Vertical

Integration" as the process of bringing every phase of producing a product under one roof. Most of the major players in today's poultry industry employ this concept that Jesse Jewell began to implement in the early fifties. But Jesse's idea to go to "bulk feed" deliveries made for a step of immense efficiency in labor and material at the time.

Chicken feed was delivered to the farm by trucks loaded with one hundred pound sacks of feed. Many farmers and feed mill workers, in their later years, would spend substantial time and money in the office of the local chiropractor for treatment for their worn out backs from lifting and moving the sacks. However, one contingency on the farm almost killed the idea of bulk feed before it got off the ground. The brightly printed cotton sacks were treasured by the farmer's wife for making dresses for herself and her daughters. The prints varied in patterns enough so that the same dress was unlikely to show up at the church picnic or family reunion. The saving of time and labor eventually overrode the demand for dress material, and bulk feed became the accepted mode of operation.

There were two recognized school systems in Hall County Georgia where the Jewell's corporate office and processing plant was domiciled. In reality, there were actually three. Hall County Schools included a number of elementary and smaller high schools scattered across one of the geographical larger counties in the state. Gainesville School System was classified as a private system although all of its employees were paid their base teacher pay by the State of Georgia. Like other small city school systems in Georgia, Gainesville had access to a broader tax base that had resulted from some creative annexing of commercial property which allowed for better facilities and state of the art athletic programs.

While the county schools could compete very successfully in the "lesser" sports like basketball or track and field, Gainesville High boasted one of the top football programs in the state. Like many small communities in the south that held the game football as a way of life, success on the gridiron was paramount to any other school or community function.

Since integration had not yet come to the South, Gainesville and Hall County officials had worked out a deal to provide educational facilities for the children of their "colored" families. The wealthier Gainesville system had constructed Fair Street Elementary and E.E. Butler High School on the south side of town adjacent to the industrial section and the majority of the African-American population. However, a few black families lived as far north as the rural community of Lula some fifteen miles north of Gainesville, and some fifteen miles south of Gainesville (which was the centrally located county seat) in the small former furniture manufacturing and cotton town of Flowery Branch. Busing was in place in Hall County long before the U.S. Supreme Court mandate. The agreement between city and county brought all the county's black students to Fair Street or E.E. Butler. The arrangement was not unusual in the South, but, unlike systems in South Georgia and states like Alabama and Mississippi, the facilities in Gainesville consisted of a lot more than clapboard buildings heated by wood or coal with outdoor restrooms.

Yet, even in Gainesville-Hall County that would by the late 60's embrace integration without much incidence there definitely existed a cultural border between black and white that, if crossed, could result in serious consequences. So when the ever popular class leader Janet Jewell, who was also the cheerleader captain, decided to invite the E.E. Butler cheerleading squad to her back yard for an afternoon of comparing notes and even sharing of gossip, some eyebrows were raised to say the least.

One of the parents who were most alarmed (the incidence caused the blood pressure of both black and white parents to rise) was Anna Lou Jewell. The mother and daughter did not get along well anyway. Janet had her dad eating out of the palm of her hand and this probably added to the friction between Anna Lou and daughter Janet. Anna Lou insisted that the invitation of the girls from across town never happen again. The Jewell family had the first and only backyard pool in town and God forbid if one of 'those girls' had decided to go swimming. When Jesse learned of the incidence he remained silent. Later, he would privately pull Janet aside and tell her that he was proud of her. Although Janet obviously had significant leverage with her dad, based on Jesse's past openness to the inclusion of black workers alongside of whites, he probably was sincere in his comments to her.

*Janet Jewell,
cheerleading captain*

CHAPTER 8

A MAN MAKES HIS PLANS BUT GOD DETERMINES HIS
STEPS — SOLOMON

The minutes of J.D. Jewell board meetings during the early and mid-fifties often recorded discussions of potential acquisitions and officer compensation. On the acquisition subject, Southern Fridge Dough Inc. of Florence, Alabama was a much sought after operation because of its potential capability of producing chicken pot pies under the Jewell logo. In the May board meeting, the purchase of additional life insurance on Jesse's life was pursued because of the insistence of the lending institutions who were supplying an ever increasing line of credit. However, a problem had arisen in the underwriting of Jesse for additional coverage. He was declined. For a man in apparent good health it was perplexing to some of the board members and lenders as to why Jesse would not be offered more coverage. If Jesse didn't qualify for standard rates then why was there not at least an offer even at a higher rating, but why a decline? The reality was that as Howard Fuller and a few close friends and family knew, and as the underwriting department at the insurance company had learned, Jesse's drinking had become more prolific. Exacerbating the problem was Jesse's ability to function at full capacity as CEO and ambassador for the company and the industry without showing any effect. There was never any indication that alcohol was impairing his judgment; however, his increasing inclination to add an array of innovative operations and products to the company's operations, and his lack of hesitancy to borrow money, may have been just as addictive. Again, most of the observations of those who knew him at the time, men like Coy Skaggs, Jack Prince and Gordon Sawyer, agree that Jesse was never greedy or even cared much for money or hoarding it. What excited him was coming up with a new idea of how to market more chicken, money was just a necessary ingredient to bring those ideas into reality. And Jesse Jewell was good at making money, and he knew that he could always make more.

At age fifteen, Tennent Lee Griffin was already a strikingly beautiful young woman who was turning the heads of the male passengers in the Crescent Line dining car. Her point of departure had been her hometown of Mobile, Alabama, where her father was respected as an affluent business man. Travel was not new to Tennent, but her mother had planned this mother-daughter trip to Washington D.C. in the spring of 1954 as a way to be with her daughter as much as possible, recognizing that leaving for college and adulthood was quickly approaching.

Both mother and daughter awkwardly hesitated in the dining car's entrance as they realized all tables were taken. Just as they turned to leave, a well-dressed man with a slight mustache stood and graciously invited them to join him at his table. Tennent's mom looked briefly at her daughter and then accepted. Tennent does not recall there being anyone else at the stranger's table. Tennent was so overwhelmed by the charm and eloquence of their host that she only remembers a delightful evening as she enjoyed the intriguing conversation between Jesse Jewell and her mom. He was ever the gentleman, even as he instructed the waiter to put all charges on his account. Mrs. Griffin however insisted that she pay for her and Tennet's dinner. The next morning, as she and her mother exited the train in Washington, Jesse bid them farewell but not before inviting them to the "Garden Spot of the South" and to tour his poultry business at their earliest convenience.

Tennent Lee Slack, as she would become known after her marriage to Bill Slack of Gainesville Georgia, would not see Jesse Jewell again until after completing her education at Vanderbilt University where she met her husband-to-be. She was impressed that not only did he recognize her several years later at a social gathering in Gainesville, but he also remembered her name and inquired about the well-being of her mother .

Jesse was traveling on to New York on business. Why he chose the train as his mode of travel is not known. He usually drove himself in his Lincoln, his automobile of choice most of his life, and Ed Jared had not yet been hired as company pilot. After Jared's arrival at J.D. Jewell Company, Jesse would travel almost exclusively with Ed at the controls in the cockpit. But his chance meeting with Tennent and her mother would leave a lasting impression on her that she fondly recalls.

The 1956 form 1040 for Jesse D. and Anna Lou Jewell showed an adjusted gross income of $67,149 and itemized deductions of $26,359. Although the sum was much greater than the average income of the day, it still was less than what many business or majority stockholders would have taken in Jesse's position. The annual amount was more than adequate to maintain the Jewell's lifestyle and still provide amenities like the backyard pool. Purchasing the home for Barbara in Arizona, sending Pat to UNC, and regular family vacations including taking domestic help along were provided by Jesse's salary and what dividends that were declared by J.D. Jewell, Inc.

In the spring of 1954, Dr. Josiah Crudup, president of Brenau College and personal friend of Jesse, announced the plans for a Home Economics building that would be named in honor of Mary Tallulah Jewell. Brenau's board of trustees agreed to match the generous contribution that Jesse had made for that year as well.

At a company board meeting in late 1954, Jack Prince reported that a contract with grocery giant A&P had been signed. Clarence Cummings brought more good news to the table as he reported on the profits of the by-products plant in Pendergrass. Although local residents continually complained about the odor filling the air in the rural community, at least there was no threats from the Environmental Protection Agency to contend with. At the same meeting, Jesse himself was able to tell the board that the newly completed feed mill had been leased to Pillsbury on very lucrative terms.

The year 1955 saw the first television appearance of Elvis and introduced Gun Smoke to Western fans. Ray Kroc would open a hamburger drive-in called McDonalds and Brooklyn Dodger fans would celebrate their team's first victory over the Yankees in the World Series. Things were going well for J.D. Jewell, Inc. as well. By 1956, the company would boast one hundred and thirty six wholesale distribution locations and nineteen thousand retail outlets. Ed Jared had come on board and the company had its first plane that Ed piloted carrying Jesse and other company executives to industry meetings and, more importantly, to customers. The purchase of an IBM 'record keeper' had the amazing capability to show almost immediate results of sales as compared to cost. In the first thirty five weeks of 1956 sales exceeded six hundred thousand pounds, already surpassing the totals of the previous year. Best of all, final year profits stood at $227,000 as compared to $36,000 in 1955. Business was so good in fact that some younger and hungrier individuals, who were watching from the sidelines, decided that there was room for some more players in the poultry industry.

Another ominous observer had been closely watching the Jewell operation as well. Late in 1956, the Board of Directors voted to assign 600 acres of land to the IRS rather than fight a tax dispute in federal court. The settlement placed the company's finances in a precarious position because the land had been used as collateral when extra cash was needed from its lenders. The effects of the IRS settlement were still being dealt with in 1957. In the May meeting of that year the Board of Directors voted to secure a loan from the Federal Land Bank, but the Land Bank required Jesse and Howard Fuller to personally guarantee the debt. The board voted unanimously to go ahead with the loan.

Far away up North in the city of Madison, Wisconsin, the excitement on the university campus could be felt in the air as students anticipated the arrival of The Platters. The popular group that had several number one hits was scheduled to perform at the spring dance which involved all sorority and fraternity members. On the Saturday evening of the dance, a young tall handsome man sporting a flat top haircut and white tuxedo escorted his date onto the dance floor. If he was not the best looking guy on campus, he still had few rivals, but without a doubt the young woman who walked at his side was the prettiest girl in Madison.

Janet Jewell wore a dress that not only was stunning but also pushed the envelope close to the edge of the school's dress code. While many of the young men gawked, most of the young women in attendance tried to appear not to notice as they masked their impunity with forced smiles. The Platters had decided to mix a Carolina beach music hit, originally performed by the Tams, as one of their selections for the evening. As the backup voices harmonized in the background, the lead singer crooned the lyrics to "Be Young, Be Foolish, But Be Happy." Later that evening Janet would take that advice as she made love with Darrell MacIntyre. Darrell had not only been mesmerized by Janet but also had fallen hopelessly in love with her. As the end of spring quarter approached, he found it almost unbearable to anticipate their parting, especially since much of Janet's summer vacation would be spent in Europe with other students. While Darrell remained in Madison completing his pre-law degree Janet arrived in London. She first tried to explain away her morning nausea as traveling sickness, which she had never experienced before. In her heart she knew the truth. A friend helped her to get an appointment at a clinic close to their hotel.

An indifferent nurse speaking in a heavy English accent, but without emotion, bluntly told nineteen year old Janet Jewell that she was pregnant. The group left London the next day and continued on schedule to Paris. The same friend, who helped her in London, had already discussed with her the option of an abortion. Although the procedure was several years from being legalized, its practice was well known in Paris. Janet made her 3:00 PM appointment for an interview located "literally in a back ally" in downtown Paris. She was instructed to return later that evening with the entire fee in cash and was assured she would be on her way by the next day "free of her burden." Janet was alone and scared. She had heard accounts of young women bleeding to death. Plus, something just didn't seem right about what she was doing.

Later in her life, Janet, who would come to be known by her stage name of Jay, would have a successful acting and business career, and even obtain a law degree and practice law as a member of the California Bar. However, the most courageous decision she would ever make was to give birth to her baby daughter Tracey. In the meantime, however, she knew she had to tell her parents. Anna Lou answered the phone and immediately asked if everything was alright. Janet, typical of her manner, was direct and to the point. Her mother was just as quick to express her anguish and immediately handed the receiver to Jesse. Jesse listened in silence as his baby daughter, now sobbing, told him of her condition. His immediate and only response was, "I love you baby, come on home and I'll take care of you."

Ed Pierce was usually a man with not much to say, but at the May meeting of the Board of Directors, his fellow board members grew quiet as he described the process of destroying several thousand company laying hens that had been infected with "New Castle" disease. The dreaded virus was feared throughout the industry and could shut down a farm, or worse, put a poultry company out of business. It was determined that although egg production would be off for a few weeks, it could recover if the disease could be held in check. Theron Brown followed with a report on the chicken pie plant in Alabama. The losses that were showing up monthly were attributed to the warehousing and shipping cost associated with the Florence pie plant. Theron suggested that the Board of Directors might consider moving the warehouse operation closer to if not to Gainesville. A lengthy discussion followed in which the minutes recorded that "all breeding and broiler growing to be in a radius 15 miles of Gainesville." It was concluded that this move would result in lower costs of chick and feed delivery, lower pick up cost and more efficient field services. It sounded like a good idea, but it was a commitment that the company could not keep. Competition for good growers would prove to be its undoing.

By September of that year, the board was deliberating on how to respond to another IRS audit. The agency had made a final offer to settle out of tax court for $230,450 .18 including $62,801 .37 in interest. Since the full amount was required before going to battle in the courtroom, the general consensus was to settle and move on. In the same meeting Jesse reported that the company's operation in Puerto Rico, "had turned out to be an unfortunate and expensive project" whose losses would also have to be absorbed along with the federal tax bill.

In the next paragraph, Jesse recommended that the company lease an airplane. He gave eight reasons why this was a viable proposal the last one being that by leasing there would be no effect on available credit. The monthly rental cost was $1,346 .89 for thirty-six months. Jesse then gave the names of individuals and firms that were also leasing their own planes including Louis Chemell. Since Ed Jared was already flying company personnel to sales and industry meetings, the plane could also be used to help Ed secure more military contracts, an already successful endeavor. There was a brief silence after Jesse's proposal until Hank Conway spoke up. It was the accountant's opinion that perhaps it would be more prudent for the company to charter a plane on an as needed basis. Again the room grew quiet. Finally, Charlie Thurmond stated, "that it was a good investment", and in his opinion the company should proceed with the lease immediately. George Van Giesen seconded Charlie's motion.

Pat Prince remembers her mom and dad being regular church attendees during her childhood, but by the time their children were coming along, her parent's church involvement was limited to some financial support. However, another Sunday ritual had become a regular routine for Jesse and Anna Lou. Usually accompanied by grandson Jesse and his older sister Debby, along with other friends and family who might show up, the family could always be found at 'their' table down at the Imperial Restaurant.

Jimmy Carras had moved from his downtown location to the popular strip of businesses located on the highway running south to Atlanta, about five miles out of town. His new restaurant offered the most upscale dining north of Atlanta. The menu offered a variety of

The Imperial was initially called Nicholson's before Ethel and Jimmy made it one of the high-end restaurants in North Georgia.

seafood and steak entrees, and of course, Southern fried chicken. Unless he was too busy, which was rare on Sunday nights, Jimmy would join the family as they finished their meal. Dessert for the grandchildren and coffee for the adults was on the house.

Culturally, Jesse and Jimmy were separated by language and custom, but perhaps because of their similar backgrounds of starting a business from scratch, the two men had a special bond between them.

Jesse had also found a true friend in his new son-in-law, Darrell MacIntyre. After their daughter was born, both Janet and Darrell had continued their education. While Janet finished an advanced degree and had joined the faculty at Gainesville College, Darrell had finished his law degree at the University of Georgia. Likeable as well as very capable, the young attorney was enjoying success in one of the more established firms in town. His work schedule though only allowed one afternoon a week to join his father-in-law in a foursome at Chattahoochee Club's course just north of town. With the addition of grandchildren from the marriages of all three of his daughters, Jesse was rich in family. Ironically, his net worth as measured by material wealth had peaked at age 55, corresponding with the apex of J.D. Jewell Inc. as well.

Max Ward's talent of growing a poultry operation was well known by now in poultry circles around North Georgia as well as the industry at large. He had represented a small group of poultry men in the purchase of Mar-Jac Poultry from Jack McKibbon Jr., who had

(left to right) Homer Wilson, Max Ward, Mark Heard, Jr., A.C. Smith

been a World War II fighter ace in the Pacific. Along with his father Jack Sr., and his uncle Marvin, McKibbon Brothers Co., would go on to build a very successful hotel business after selling out to the Ward group in December of 1959. By the early sixties, Max Ward and the companies that he was affiliated with would grow to one of the largest concerns in the industry.

To the north of Gainesville, the Folger family had established a significant foothold in the broiler market under the leadership of Tom and his brother. As mentioned earlier,

Tom Arrendale and Joe Hatfield were emerging as industry giants.

Ground breaking for Mar-Jac that was eventually purchased by Max Ward. (left to right) Emerson Stowe, Jack McKibbon, Sr., Marvin McKibbon, Jack McKibbon, Jr.

Although Jesse was agreeably recognized as the original pioneer of the chicken business that same fame failed to give him and his company any advantage with prospective customers or suppliers. Like everyone else, he had to earn his way each day. The past was nice to recall, but the future belonged to the man who could not only sell the most chicken, but sell it at a profit.

Jack Prince listed ten primary markets for the Jewell Company during the July 1957 board meeting. The list included names like Swanson, Safeway Stores, and National Tea and concluded with the categories of T.V. Dinners, Precook, and the disappearing Ice Pack market. While the atmosphere at most meetings was not formal, the typical hour long sessions were run in a business-like manner with Jesse presiding unless he happened to be out of town .

However, the mood at the August, 1957 meeting could best be described as tense. As Jesse read a typed resolution into the minutes, everyone avoided eye contact with Howard Fuller. Although it would now be official, everyone knew that accountant and comptroller Hank Conway was gone. The resolution concluded with the transferring of a company owned life insurance policy to Mr. Conway as part of his severance.

At issue was the taking of a $250,000 loan from the Teachers Retirement System of Georgia that Charlie Thurmond had been working on for some time. Hank Conway had not been shy in voicing his objection to the company taking on additional debt, preferring rather to cutting cost and "doing away with some frills." On the Saturday morning prior to the board meeting, Jesse had driven to the company's offices which were still at the Maple Street location. He knew that most likely, Hank would be there as he was most Saturdays. Conway was a hardworking and dedicated employee, but he often butted heads with Jesse over spending money. Jesse had his faults, but a bad temper was not considered one of them. However, this morning he had been drinking. Whether it impaired his judgment, no one would ever know. The details of the conversation were never discussed by either man, but when Jesse left, Hank Conway no longer had a job with J.D. Jewell Inc.

When Howard Fuller heard of Hank's firing he also made a difficult but decisive decision. Howard not only was fond of the company's in-house comptroller, but found that he more times than not agreed with his frugal recommendations and assessments. Jesse was his longtime friend but the more progressive board members now had his ear. It was time for Howard to get out. Again, no one knows how the conversation went, but if the mood of the meeting when Hank Conway's departure was announced was tense, then the mood of the meeting which followed in September could only be described as somber. Howard had provided much of the money to start the company back in 1946. The terms that Charlie Thurmond read to the rest of the board to buy Howard out made everyone aware that it was going to be expensive, but no one objected. The terms included, along with cash, a sizeable amount of preferred stock and the real estate that housed the company offices. Once the motion was made and seconded, it was approved unanimously. There being no further business, the meeting was adjourned. One observer recalled only that Jesse's eyes "watered up" as he left. It would be the second defining moment in the life of the company, the first one being the decision to go strictly frozen product. But unlike the first decision, this one would have minimal impact on the poultry industry. The Industry was so big now it would not miss the demise of one company even if it was its first and most famous one.

Poultry Parade in Downtown Gainesville in Poultry's Heyday

Jesse cuts the cake at a birthday party for his mother, Tallulah Dickson Jewell. (l-r) Jesse Jewell, Ed Jewell, Tallulah Dickson Jewell, Edith Lily Jewell, Mary Loudermilk, unknown, Joe Sharp, Iola Mae Loudermilk Sharp, Anna Lou Jewell, Leonard Parks, Jay MacIntosh (Janet Jewell), Homer Sharp, Jr., Barbara Jewell, Ed Parks, Sr., Ruby Loudermilk Parks

CHAPTER 9

KNOW WELL THE CONDITIONS OF YOUR FLOCKS... FOR
RICHES ARE NOT FOREVER — SOLOMON

Along with being the first grower for Jesse Jewell, the Stowe family had a unique history with some of the industry's most notable names. Bill Jr. would work alongside Lloyd Strickland manually packing eggs at Gold Kist. Bill recalls that the man, who would become one of the egg industry's legends, was friendly but quiet, and a very hard worker. After returning from military service, Bob Hamrick, future mayor of Gainesville, hired Bill Jr. to work in the picking room at the Jewell plant. The work was dirty but not near as grungy as the men who worked in the eviscerating area where the 'birds' arrived on trucks from the farms.

Twenty four squawking chickens were hung feet first on shackles and then proceeded to have their throats cut. The process required great precision to allow proper bleed out without bruising the meat. At exactly 124 degrees, the birds were scalded to remove the feathers.

If the job title of eviscerator was unclear to someone outside the industry, then a simple observation of the eviscerator's white apron at the end of the workday would not leave much to the imagination as to what he had been doing all day. Bill Jr. would advance quickly at J.D. Jewell Inc. and leave the company in 1967 for a high management position with another poultry processor. A third generation Stowe, Bill III, continues the family tradition today as plant manager for King's Delight, one of the industry's mega firms.

So, Bill Jr's perspective really covers many of the years that the poultry industries were in transformation from locally owned companies to the huge publicly held giants of today. In retrospect, he continues to hold Jesse Jewell as the industry's most influential and important leader. Yet, during his last days with the company, he could tell something wasn't right. It was hard for him to identify the problem at the time, looking back he's convinced that there may have been "too many chiefs for the number of Indians."

Skip Hope worked for the Jewell Company throughout his high school and college years during the summer months between spring and fall quarters. Except for the two years he served on the USS Franklin D. Roosevelt, all of his work experience was with the Jewell Company. Bob Hamrick, personnel manager, had noticed Skip's ability to handle more complex tasks than the cutting line required. Since Skip's major was accounting, it was a practical move to promote the young accountant to work with now company comptroller Ben Carter. Skip recalls his early years of meeting and knowing Jesse Jewell as being mostly in a state of awe. Mr. Jewell was friendly to everyone and would even take time to stop by Skip's cubicle and talk for a moment. The morning after North Carolina won the 1958 NCAA tournament, Mr. Jewell, knowing that Skip was a college basketball fan, asked him what he thought of the game. Skip remembers sensing that the boss was sincerely interested in what he had to say.

Bob Hamrick also has only positive comments about his legendary boss. On more than one occasion, Mr. Jewell would quietly suggest that his young Georgia Tech graduate personnel manager give some down-on-his-luck local fellow a job "Ah, you can find something for him to do" he would admonish Bob, grinning as he left Bob with the responsibility of finding a place for the unemployed man or woman.

Although "generous to a fault", Bob Hamrick, Skip Hope and others who knew Jesse Jewell would not even come close to describing him as a foolish spendthrift. He just had a confidence about himself that he even passed on to those around him, that the company could always make more money as it was needed. Both men agree however, along with Coy Skaggs, that if Jesse had a fault other than being too generous, it was that he trusted some folks that he probably shouldn't have.

On any given day in 1959, when Jesse left home to travel to the company offices, his route would have taken him just over three miles. The family now lived at 965 Green St. Circle, one of Gainesville's older and quainter neighborhoods. Originally, the house would not have been described as huge but spacious enough to accommodate the friends and growing number of grandchildren who were frequently found there. Pulling onto Green Street and traveling south towards downtown, huge homes, built by some of the city's most affluent families just

Jesse and Anna Lou on the back steps of their Green Street Circle home

before and after the turn of the century, lined both sides of the town's most distinguished street. The elegant old two wide porches and three story houses with tall, white columns can be seen today, much the same as they appeared to Jesse on his way to work.

Jesse had basically two approaches to his office. The most direct route would have taken him down Academy Street, past the rear of the old Gainesville High School building and gymnasium, on out towards the mill village of Gainesville Mill and one of several choices of streets to his right and southwest to the plant and offices across from the Gainesville airport.

If however, he had reason to go through downtown in his Lincoln, he would have approached the square traveling south on Main Street. In the late 50's and early 60's, Gainesville, Georgia, really had a "Norman Rockwell look" to its downtown, and some of the surrounding residential communities. As Jesse came to the intersection of Main and Washington Streets, "Old Joe", the Confederate soldier memorial that had survived the '36 tornado, would be at his post facing north. Woolworth and McClellan dime stores were separated by Washington Street, Woolworth's on the north corner and McClellan's on the south.

Woolworth housed a lunch counter that served a toasted bun slaw dog rivaled only by the ones served at the Collegiate a block south on Main. McClellan's response to the competition was a candy counter with every form of chocolate covered nut and raisins, tempting shoppers from behind the glass shielded trays that were approximately eye level to the average nine or ten year old.

Circling the square, Jesse could have stopped at the Dixie Hunt for lunch. To reach the dining room, he would have walked passed Mr. Myron Lackie's barber shop, equipped with six ornate barber chairs and a raised shoeshine station staffed by a black gentleman who had probably been there faithfully for thirty years. Three soda shops, located in three different drug stores, offered Jesse another choice for a BLT or milkshake made in noisy tin canisters spinning and mixing hand dipped ice cream with milk and chocolate.

Saul's department store, which faced north on Spring Street, competed with the J.C. Penney and Gallant Belk's chains located at opposite corners of the square. Ironically, Lorry Schrage continues today to successfully operate the business founded by his parents in 1936 as his competitors have moved on to busier and impersonal malls. Completing the circle of the downtown square, Jesse would have stopped often at the Frierson-McEver men's clothing store to pick up a shirt or maybe one of the Hart Shafter & Marx suits that professionals and business owners, both locally and from points north, traveled to for the top lines of dress and casual clothing.

The Royal Theatre was just off the square adjacent to the Dixie Hunt and facing Main Street. Across from the Royal, Western Auto offered an assortment of auto accessories along with the latest models of Schwin bicycles, which made the store a popular place around Christmas. The only other sporting goods store in town, and North Georgia, was Lewis Tate's Outdoor Shop which offered everything from basketballs to Browning shotguns.

The three main denominations of the Bible belt were represented in large brick edifices just off the square. Although the First Baptist Church was destroyed by fire the First Methodist and First Presbyterians would not move to the suburbs until later in the decade.

On the surface, Gainesville appeared as the all-American town. But all was not as simple and innocent as it might have been seen by the casual observer. And just a mile or so away, not all was well at the J .D .Jewell Company either.

"I know we pay our growers more and our plant help more than our competition. I'm not sure you could call it a weakness but it does affect the bottom line. But I started with these people and grew up in the business with them, and I'm going to continue to give them every break I can afford to give them."—Jesse Jewell-1959.

During a plant opening in 1950 attended by a host of local dignitaries and representatives from the Georgia Department of Agriculture, Jesse had to fill in at one point on the program for a local politician who had fallen ill just prior to the ceremony. Without any preparation or notes, Jesse spellbound the audience, first with his impromptu humor, then his optimistic outlook for the future of the business and the industry followed by a brief message of appreciation to the folks who had made the plant possible—his employees.

Jesse had the gift of capturing a crowded room as he entered, but at the same time, making the individual feel comfortable and important, and that Jesse was sincerely listening to what that person was saying. Rarely did anyone see him lose his temper. Impulsive as he was, he never was offensive or condescending. Ed Jared recalls a conversation between Jesse and Joe DiMaggio while Ed was flying the two men to several locations around the country to call on customers. Mr. DiMaggio had been contracted through his agent on several occasions to help promote and market J.D. Jewell products. Somehow, the subject of Marilyn Monroe had come up as Joe was describing his ex-wife. After listening for a few minutes, Jesse asked Joe why the marriage hadn't worked out. Joe seemed stunned, and while he remained silent searching for an answer, Jesse continued," Well I sure wish ya'll could have made it, she seems like a fine lady to me." The discussion about his ex was over and Joe started talking about baseball.

Joe DiMaggio and Ed Jared

Company promotional tour: Jesse Jewell (2nd from left), Joe DiMaggio (3rd from left)

The regular board meeting of the Jewell Company started promptly at 3:00 PM on the afternoon of 24 February, 1959. Jesse had been frustrated by the habit of late arrival of several of his top executives on the board and had instituted a policy that "if a man is late, he forfeits his director check."

The first topic on the agenda was the follow up discussion on a new product packaging being designed by Royal Dadum Company and produced by Austill Paper Company. Then the discussion turned to more serious matters which started with the closing of the Toccoa plant. This was followed with more sobering news reported by Ben Carter that the Company was currently operating at a $26,000 per month net loss. Jesse encouraged his team to sell more chicken and pointed out that the plant had the capacity to produce 600,000 pounds of products without increasing labor or machinery which would result in a $10,760 monthly net profit. While the Board members agreed by affirmative nods of their heads, no one brought up the possibility of reducing some of the expenses except Ben Carter.

The Company had taken over the management and operation of the Dixie Hunt Hotel which was owned by Brenau College. Jesse had agreed to the arrangement after some of the college officials had come to him for help in operating what had become a financial albatross. The ever generous Jesse had agreed to help the school out, seeking the approval of his board after the fact.

Ed Jared had been summoned to Jesse's office on the morning after the deal with Brenau had been reached The company pilot, who had by now began to register some marked success in military sales of the Jewell products, was informed by his boss that he was the new general manager of North Georgia's largest hotel. Ed would find that his considerable flying skills, his past record of flying combat missions over "The Hump", along with his natural sales ability, would all fail him as he attempted to rescue the faltering hotel. By now it was obvious that Jesse should do what he knew best and stay out of the hotel business. The losses were totaling a staggering $40,000 per month. The only suggestion recorded in the minutes by another attending board member was that of now president Charlie Thurmond. Charlie asked if a lower lease payment from Brenau might be a possibility. The question went unanswered as the other board members remained silent.

Another non-poultry enterprise that had been acquired by the company was also struggling and adding to the loss of revenue. Jewell Motors, which had been the name picked for the Lincoln-Mercury dealership after its acquisition, was losing almost as much money as the Hunt. It was decided to separate from the hotel and to sell the car dealership. It would be only a few months later that the same action would be taken for Southern Fridge Dough Inc. Even though the Florence, Alabama pre-prepared bakery had a closer link to poultry than hotels or auto dealerships, it too had proven to be a consistent loser.

Ironically, the most profitable operation under the Jewell umbrella was its least glamorous. Georgia Tech graduate Haskell Stratton was running the offal plant in Pendergrass, Georgia at a handsome profit. The former army paratrooper's day started at about 5:00 a. m. at the plant some fifteen miles south of his home in Gainesville. By 5:00 p. m. he would return home to eat supper with his wife and see his small children off to bed. On many nights, Haskell would be called back to the plant when some of the cooking vats holding hundreds of gallons of blood and chicken waste would break down. Haskell gave 14 years of his working life to the effort.

*A load of offal arriving at the Jewell Plant
in Pendergrass*

Adding to some of the Company's woes, several good men were leaving to start their own business. Theron Brown went to Atlanta and started a successful food brokerage operation, and continued to help the Jewell Company place chicken into several new markets.

Another man who also left Jesse on good terms and remained friends would attain business success recognized on a national and international level. Jimmy Wilkins, who had graduated from Georgia Tech with a degree in engineering, had built a thriving argyle sock manufacturing plant in the rural north Georgia town of Helen. When some large manufacturers picked up on the success of Wilkins, they began to enter the game with unlimited resources for machines and capital. Wilkins saw that the stylish men's socks, like any fashion, would someday end. He wisely decided not to make the investment into plant and machinery facilities to compete with the bigger players.

The Wilkins and Jewells were close friends, having met at the Chattahoochee Country Club during golf tournaments and social events. Jesse had offered Wilkins a position that used both his people management skills and his sales and marketing expertise to promote chicken. Three years after Wilkins started, a fire destroyed part of the facility that housed the majority of his activities. Rather than wait for the rebuilding of a new building, Wilkins returned to Helen and started managing a mid-range women's clothing plant. Within a decade the company boasted eleven additional plants located in small towns of north Georgia and North Carolina.

Most of the employees were women who were allowed in some instances, to take cloth home and sew on their own sewing machine. All of Wilkins' work force lived in rural southern Appalachia where opportunities for well-paying jobs were rare, especially for women. Orbit Manufacturing, the official corporate name for all of the Wilkins' plants, offered many mothers, often times, single moms, opportunity to bring home extra income to feed, clothe and educate their children. The company was a classic family owned business. Wilkins and his wife, Betsy, worked side by side, and later all four sons would be strategically placed to grow the business. Jesse and Wilkins would remain friends until Jesse's death.

Two decades would pass before the textile industry of the South would begin the exit to offshore manufacturing. By the time it took place, the Wilkins family fortune would be well established and secured. However, competition in the poultry business was intensifying regionally and nationally. Joe Hatfield and the Arrendale brothers were well on their way to building their conglomerate. They would eventually make an offer to the Folger family whose operation in Murrayville, Georgia had been very successful. The Folgers accepted the offer, which would allow Tom and his brother a little more time on the golf course and relief from their accustomed, twelve hour workday.

Jesse took note of the growing industry around him that he was credited with starting twenty five years earlier. He recognized that he would have to compete on more than just his well-known and respected name. In an attempt to keep his company viable and current, he tried to find and hire capable people. If Jesse had one glaring weakness in business, it was in this arena. His trusting nature and inclination to want people to like him meant that he would be inclined to overlook incompetence and give too many second chances. Perhaps his firing of Hank Conway and the departure of Howard Fuller had made him weary of making necessary management changes.

A manager for the Pendergrass offal plant had come on board and immediately recommended the implementation of a costly continuous cook process over the batch cook which had been working so well. No one bothered to ask Haskell Stratton who had been running the plant at a good profit. The final board meeting of 1959 was held on 3 December at 2:00 p.m. The financial picture that was presented was as dark gray as the winter day outside. Low sales, it was concluded, was the problem. Jack Prince had begun to see that perhaps the financial stress that the company was experiencing may have been due more to some "unnecessary" spending and high salaries among the management group. But not only was he the youngest man on the board, he was Jesse's son-in-law. Although reluctant to say anything, he began to see that the future could prove to be difficult if some changes were not made.

Jesse and Anna Lou at one of the many poultry
industry events honoring his legacy

J. D. Jewell Company Board of Directors in the late 1950's or early 1960's: (left to right) Carl Cochin, President of Lockheed Georgia; Carter Estes; unidentified; Charles Thurmond, President Elect; Jesse Jewell, Board Chairman; George Van Geisen, Vice President; Carl Chandler, Board Chairman Standard Packaging Corp.; unidentified; Clarence Cummings, By Products Division President; Tom McGough, Southern Frigid Dough, Inc. of Florence, Alabama

CHAPTER 10

I NEVER MET A MAN WHO DIDN'T THINK HE HAD AT
LEAST ANOTHER 20 YEARS — MARK TWAIN

Rebecca Louise Burnette had been born in 1956 as one of the three grandchildren from the union of Jack and Pat Prince. The family home address was 115 Piedmont Avenue, which was just steps away from grandparents, Jesse and Anna Lou. Rebecca (Becky) and big sister Debby spent most of the days they were out of school at the grandparent's back yard pool. Anna Lou always prepared lunch on Mondays and mandatory attendance was expected for any family in proximity of Gainesville. Becky remembers her grandmother's brownies as the best she ever ate. Often, they were enjoyed with a glass of milk while sitting in her grandfather's lap as he watched the Merv Griffin Show. The children always entered their grandparent's home through the kitchen where the aroma coming from Anna Lou's white porcelain stove would give them a hint of what treat lay ahead. Favorites, along with the infamous brownies, included divinity, peanut brittle, and ice cream made with Heath Bars. Jesse was a good grandfather. The same charisma and sense of humor that had won over many of Jesse's customers over the years, he now employed to entertain and spoil his grandchildren. He had always enjoyed cooking steaks for guests on the outside charcoal grill by the pool. With the same zeal, he now used his self-proclaimed chef skills to grill burgers and hot dogs for the grandchildren. If business was not going as well as he would have liked at the plant and office, it didn't seem to impair his passion for enjoying his wife, children and grandchildren.

Jesse was not a perfect husband. After being confronted by Anna Lou of an indiscretion that had come to her knowledge, Jesse made reservations at the exclusive Cloister at Sea Island, Georgia. The former vacation abode for some of America's richest families provided a romantic back drop for Jesse to make amends. While out dining at the resort's formal restaurant, Jesse had the bathtub in their suite filled with rose petals to surprise Anna Lou upon their return, proving that his gift for creativity was not limited to selling chickens.

Both Anna Lou and Jesse enjoyed fishing.

Jesse Jewell counted several men as close friends and confidantes during his lifetime. Conrad Romberg and Coy Skaggs were always ready to listen to Jesse on business matters. His old friend Jimmy Carras could always be counted on to listen to and encourage him when he was down or discouraged. And while his departure from the company had strained their communication, Jesse knew that Howard Fuller would faithfully be available if he really needed him.

Jimmy Caras in later years

So, it remains a mystery to this day as to how and why Jesse came to the decision to sell his business. Of the friends and family who were interviewed for this writing, none recall of there being any hint of Jesse's intentions. Pat Prince is convinced that not even her mother nor any other family member had any idea of what Jesse was contemplating. Most conclude however that even though Jesse could be impulsive at times, he had probably started thinking about selling after he met Carl Chandler.

Chandler was a Georgia native who had quickly climbed a steep ladder of success in the business circles of New York's corporate community. During his ascension, he had served on the boards of several publicly held companies. He also was credited by some with closing down Collier Magazine while serving as the CEO and publisher.

Regardless of one's opinion of him, his ability to drop names of the wealthy and influential people he knew was impressive. Chandler could be perceived as being very self-confident or arrogant, depending on whom you asked. When Chandler began his role as CEO of J.D. Jewell Inc., Skip Hope had been working for only a few months in the accounting department, under the tutelage of Ben Carter. Skip recalls Chandler as a man who kept you at arm's length, but he was always fair and respectful to subordinates. Other management personnel with the company at the time would disagree.

When Haskell Stratton was fired for questioning the workability of the continuous cooking process over batch cooking at the offal plant, he left quietly without complaint. Years later he still refused to say anything at all, positive or negative about Carl Chandler. However, later, Haskell would only simply point out that as soon as the continuous process broke down, the only source for consistent profit for the company ceased as well.

Bob Fowler was probably one of the brightest and most articulate men to ever work for the Jewell Company. He left Jewell Inc. not long after Chandler's takeover when Jimmy

Wilkins called and invited him to Helen to become the general manager of his sewing plants. Fowler too has little to say about Chandler except to point out that while he was proud to have worked for Jesse Jewell, after the change, it was no longer the place he wanted to be. He was actually planning to start his own business when he got the call from Wilkins.

Incidentally, just a few years later, sitting in Paul's Steak House, overlooking the Chattahoochee River as it exits the south end of Helen, and having lunch with Wilkins and his friend Pete Hodgkinson, the three businessmen would originate and eventually implement the transformation of Helen, Georgia, from a small rural mountain town to a mega tourist attraction with an Alpine theme. Such an improvising and creative acumen would have been very timely for the Jewell Company as Chandler started his tenure. The terms of the entire deal were never really disclosed. Jesse received, what was considered at the time, a large sum of cash. But most of the payment to Jesse was made in non-voting preferred stock, essentially removing any control from him to Chandler and the board whose members Chandler had appointed. Jesse would make what would prove to be an ill-timed and over-aggressive investment into the stock market. Still, with the dividends from the stock, and a small director's fee, Jesse and Anna Lou were able to, at least initially, maintain their accustomed standard of living.

If the fifties were the years when "Father Knows Best", then the sixties would become the decade best described by James Dobson as, "When America forgot how to blush." As dogs were trained on civil rights marchers in Selma, the bulging baby boomers would soon begin to proclaim their revolution of nonconformance by conforming to bell bottoms and long hair. The flat top would disappear and along with it, the men's barbershops, marked by their candy striped barber poles and shoe shine stands. But as the tremors of change began to shake the country, some semblance of innocence, albeit superficial, would linger for at least a few years.

In 1962, Roger Marris would set a new single season home run record, (without any substance enhanced assistance), Alabama would finally overcome the bias of the national sports media to win just one of several NCAA titles for the Bear, and Gary Player would win the Masters. The Dick Van Dyke show was slowly edging out Milton Berle for the number one evening programming spot still viewed on mostly black and white television screens.

Although the schools and many other public and private institutions in the South, and much of the country remained under official or just implied segregation, African-Americans were finding it much easier to find jobs beyond the traditional agricultural or janitorial roles most often afforded them. This was especially true in the now expanding poultry industry in and around Gainesville. Even though there were no "Whites Only" or "Colored Section" signs officially drawing the lines, blacks would not be found at the all-white Royal Theater just off the Gainesville square, nor would any whites dare venture to the Roxy located a few blocks south of town. But the Jewell Company needed workers and so did its competitors. Not too far away in neighboring Alabama, a young pastor, originally from Atlanta, was courageously preaching a Gandhi style non-violent protest that would eventually change the racial landscape after his assassination.

Sadly ironic, the institution he heralded from, the American church, would remain as the nation's most segregated institution. Jesse Jewell's generation could only watch with their mouths agape in shock as the world and culture they had known was quickly slipping into history. They had defeated Hitler and the Emperor's Imperial Army, but even they could not stop or slow down the coming change, even if they had wanted to, which some to their credit did not.

Jesse Jewell had never had any interest or involvement in politics. If he had an opinion on what was being reported each evening by TV news first famous news anchors Chet Huntley and David Brinkley, he never bothered to express it. He was a business man and now that he had sold that, he had no place to go or reason to be there. More and longer trips to visit daughter Barbara and her husband Dick, and child in Arizona were filling the schedule of Jesse and Anna Lou.

February was Jesse and Anna Lou's favorite time to visit Barbara and her husband, and of course the grandchild. Jesse liked the shortest month of the year because the typical north Georgia Februaries were cold and wet with short days. In Arizona, he could play golf almost daily which he usually did. Anna Lou was not hard to please as long as she had Jesse and her children and grandchildren around.

On the eventful morning of Jesse's stroke, he had played a full eighteen holes with some golfing friends at the local club. Anna Lou was to pick him up after he had lunched with his foursome. As she pulled up at the club entranceway, Jesse was standing staring off into the distance. At first, she didn't notice anything different about her husband of almost thirty five years, assuming that he was watching an airplane on the horizon. After taking longer than usual to place his clubs in the trunk, Jesse was also uncharacteristically quiet. Again, Anna Lou was not alarmed, thinking that perhaps he had not played well, or just as likely, had played well and was going back over his game in his mind. But when they arrived at the condo that the couple had purchased for their frequent trips West, Jesse would not get out of the car. Anna Lou began to sense something was wrong.

Except for his self-imposed bouts with alcohol, her husband had rarely missed a day of work from sickness since the day they had married. Finally as she started in to call Barbara, she looked back to see Jesse fall forward on his face as he tried to emerge from the passenger side. Jesse was Anna Lou's life. She had dedicated her life to giving birth to his children, preparing his meals, and being his life mate. Her hobbies, her social life, and her existence all centered around Jesse. At first, the terror in her heart would not allow her to scream.

When her voice finally came out she heard herself crying, "Jesse! Jesse!" A belligerent neighbor who had previously observed Jesse when he had had too much to drink, opened his door only to quickly slam it shut as he muttered, "He's just drunk." Finally, a Hispanic yardman who Jesse had befriended and knew on first a name basis helped get him out of the street and then called an ambulance.

Pat would first learn of her father's stroke when Barbara called from a Tucson hospital. The always steady and calm Pat immediately filled the role of the oldest child and big sister. She and Jack took the next flight out of Atlanta leaving Debby, Jesse and Becky with trusted friends Matt and Jean Matthews. Once in Arizona, Pat took charge. Around the clock care was established and the best medical staff available was assembled with the help of Jesse's personal doctor back in Gainesville. Jesse would remain in Arizona for almost six weeks before he was medically released to travel home.

Pat had arranged for nursing and in-home assistance along with a strenuous rehabilitation program. It would not be long before he would recover his speech and mental clarity to pre-stroke levels, but Jesse Jewell would walk with the assistance of a cane for the remainder of his life.

Mary and Jack McKibbon with Anna Lou and Jesse Jewell
(1960)
Notice the cane Jesse always used after his stroke.

GEORGIA POULTRY HALL OF FAME CONTRIBUTORS

JESSE D. JEWELL — FIRST HONOREE

Associated Industries of Georgia, Atlanta
Rafe Banks, Jr., Gainesville
Rafe Banks, Sr., Gainesville
Best Ice & Locker, Gainesville
Bio-Lab, Decatur
Julius Bishop, Athens
D. W. Brooks, Atlanta
Brown-Gay, Inc., Atlanta
Brown's Ledbrest, Springdale, Ark.
Phil Campbell, Atlanta
Chestnut Mountain Hatchery, Chestnut Mt.
City Ice Company, Gainesville
Harry Crawford and Associates, Atlanta
Daily Times, Gainesville
Day, Reynolds & Parks, Gainesville
Dixieland Hatcheries, Gainesville
Leslie B. Eddington, Richmond, Va.
First Federal Savings & Loan, Gainesville
First National Bank, Gainesville
Folger Poultry Farm, Dahlonega
Floors, Inc., Atlanta
R. F. Frazier, Richmond, Va.
Gainesville Elks Lodge, Gainesville
Gainesville Fuel Co., Gainesville
Gainesville National Bank, Gainesville
Georgia Broilers, Gainesville
Georgia Chicks, Cartersville
Georgia Poultry Federation, Gainesville
Georgia Poultry Improvement Assn., Oakwood
Georgia Poultry Processors Assn., Gainesville
Georgia Power Company, Gainesville
Byron P. Harris, Atlanta
Harrold's Hatchery, Winterville
Holiday Inn, Gainesville
Holly Farms Poultry, Wilkesboro, N.C.
Home Federal Savings & Loan, Gainesville
Elizabeth Hughes, Athens

Ideal By-Products, Lawrenceville
Institute of American Poultry Industries, Chicago, Ill.
A. Carl Kotchian, Los Angeles, California
C. Ken Laurent, Bogota, Colombia, South America
W. I. Lavery, Danville, Illinois
W. L. Lawson & Son, Canton
Marbut Milling Company, Augusta
McCarty Enterprises, Magee, Mississippi
Milner's, Gainesville
National Finance Company, Gainesville
North Georgia Veterinary Supplies, Gainesville
W. L. Norton, Gainesville
Pilgrim-Estes, Gainesville
Pillsbury Company, Gainesville
Pillsbury Company, Minneapolis, Minn.
Ralston Purina, Gainesville
Rockingham Poultry, Broadway, Va.
Ruskin-Pearson Company, Atlanta
Salsbury Labs, Charles City, Iowa
Security Mills, Knoxville, Tenn.
A. C. Smith, Cumming
Sidney O. Smith, Gainesville
Southern Bell Telephone & Telegraph, Gainesville
Southern Crate & Veneer, Macon
Standard Feed Mills, Gainesville
Stone Mountain Grit, Stone Mountain
Tri-County Hatchery, Royston
Trust Company of Georgia, Atlanta
Paul Turner, Gainesville
Union Bag-Camp Paper Company, Savannah
George Van Giesen, Gainesville
Vantress Farms, Duluth
Washie Wallis, Gainesville
WDUN, Gainesville
WGGA, Gainesville
Henry Ward, Gainesville

*Display in the Northeast Georgia History Museum
referencing the Poultry Hall of Fame*

CHAPTER 11

AS FOR MAN, HIS DAYS ARE LIKE GRASS; AS A FLOWER
OF THE FIELD, SO HE FLOURISHES. WHEN THE WIND
HAS PASSED OVER IT, IT IS NO MORE, AND ITS PLACE
ACKNOWLEDGES IT NO LONGER — SOLOMON

On a hot July morning in 1962, a poultry farmer walked through one of his three hundred foot long broiler houses, picking up the dead chickens that had smothered to death the night before. Mortality rates in the flocks had been greatly improved over the past ten years, but still a marauding fox or neighbor's dog could cause a panic in the long rectangular houses, sending the chickens piling on top of each other and suffocating those on the bottom of the pile.

Even though he had been growing chickens for years, the stifling vapor of ammonia still took the farmer's breath away at times, reminding him of the days when the houses had to have the layers of wood shavings and droppings removed with a pitchfork. Thankfully, small tractors with loading buckets had replaced the back aching labor of the pitchforks. The procedure was necessary between each grow out to prevent disease, but it also made the house bearable for the farmer to enter for watering and feeding his flocks.

By the time he threw the last dead chicken onto the bed of the trailer hitched to his 8N Ford tractor, sweat had soaked through the back of his khaki work shirt. As he emerged out of the chicken house and drew a chest full of fresh air, he noticed the faded sign with the letters of the J.D. Jewell company jingle that his fieldman had given him when he first contracted to grow with Jewell. He had heard the jingle played and sung on WDUN Radio hundreds of times and the tune silently played in his head:

"Jesse Jewell frozen fresh chicken, Jesse Jewell sure is great. Jesse Jewell frozen fresh chicken, finest frozen chicken you ever ate."

The farmer could have been in the hills of Habersham or Dawson counties or the flat farmland of Barrow or Jackson County. Where his farm was is not important, but what was significant was what he did next. Pausing where he stood, he leaned his arm against the chicken house and bowed his head. With closed eyes, he silently prayed. First, he prayed a prayer of thanksgiving to God for providing him the resources to get into the chicken business. Although he was paid well for his "day" job, the extra income from poultry had enabled him to pay the tuition for his daughter to complete her teaching degree at North Georgia College.

In retrospect, the chicken houses had probably been the only way he could have held onto the farm that had been passed down from his grandfather. Lastly, he prayed for Jesse Jewell. Although he had only met the poultry industry's pioneer on limited occasions, he respected and appreciated the man who seemed genuinely friendly and attentive during their brief conversations. The farmer had heard about the stroke from another grower who had gotten the news from his fieldman. He concluded his prayer by simply asking God to place his healing and comforting hand on Mr. Jewell and his family.

Jesse's sale of the business had greatly limited his input into the management of his company, but the stroke effectively ended any future involvement in deciding the direction of the company. Carl Chandler was calling those shots now, and calling them in a grandiose way.

Although Bob Small had been originally hired as plant engineer, he also inherited the position of company pilot. Like Ed, Bob had gotten his flight training and hours while serving in the military. However, unlike Army Air Corp veteran Jared, Bob had been a Navy pilot. It didn't matter to Chandler where Bob learned to fly. What was of much more importance was that he now referred to Bob as his personal pilot, or at least that was the way Chandler introduced Bob while on trips to industry conventions or customer meetings.

Chandler was a regular customer at Frierson-McEver often explaining that he rarely wore a white dress shirt more than twice before throwing it away. His wardrobe also included the most exclusive lines of dress suits and casual wear. If Jesse Jewell's entrance had attracted the attention of the dining guests at the Chattahoochee Country Club, then Carl Chandler demanded it.

While Jesse had been known to walk through the processing plant and talk with employees on the cutting line, Chandler rarely went in the plant and never talked with anyone much below his rank. Jesse had never been one to force himself into a conversation at the Club, but Chandler would often sit down without invitation and begin to tell of his previous business accomplishments and drop the name of the affluent and famous people he knew. Ironically, the two men were hardly ever seen together after the sale, and after the stroke, never.

As Jesse's health improved, he began to make weekly visits to the Jewell offices which were now located adjacent to the processing plant. Anna Lou would drop him off about an hour before lunch and pick him up shortly after 1:30 p .m.

Carl Chandler was never available to go to lunch, so at first some of the other top management would carry Jesse. This soon became a burden for some of Jesse's old management team who seemed to always have a conflict on the days that Jesse came by. The task of getting Jesse in and out of the car and into the restaurant was delegated to some of the lower ranking managers.

Several of these men including Skip Hope and Jan Cooley jumped at the chance to take Jesse Jewell to lunch. Skip, whose duties were intensifying with the exit of senior accounting staff, fondly recalls taking Mr. Jewell to the Imperial where Jesse would be hugged and greeted by his old friend Jimmy Carras. Jimmy would always join Jesse at his table while he waited for his usual meal which featured a small Delmonico steak followed by Ethel's famous apple pie with vanilla ice cream.

Skip rarely contributed to the conversation as the two friends exchanged news about family and other old friends. Like Skip, Jan Cooley rarely became involved in the lunch conversation between Mr. Carras and Mr. Jewell. But Jan had other motives. When the opportunity was provided Jan would "pick Mr. Jewell's brain." Years later, after Cooley became one of the industry's giants, he would credit those conversations with Jesse Jewell with a large part of his personal success.

Jesse's lunch guests, however, were not limited to the junior managers of the company. Coy Skaggs, who by now was in senior management with Pillsbury, would make time to be with his friend. Coy recalls probably the last time he had lunch with Jesse in about 1969. One of the industry's most influential leaders, Abit Massey, head of the Georgia Poultry Association, had accompanied Coy on the occasion. Jesse's health had seemed to be gradually worsening, so Coy discreetly offered to cut up Jesse's steak for him. As Jesse agreed, Coy noticed the tears in the eyes of Jimmy Carras as he momentarily excused himself to take care of some matters in the kitchen. The muscles in the side of Jesse's face had weakened which meant that as he tried to chew his food, it would sometimes appear in the corner of his mouth. It wasn't long before Anna Lou would refuse to take him, feeling that it was too humiliating for him, but she would allow for old friends to visit. One of those old friends, who showed on a regular basis, bringing newspapers and magazines, was Howard Fuller.

Other friends and former employees would visit or at least try to stay in touch with Jesse. A get well note followed by a phone call of encouragement was sent by Ben and Bonnie Rucker. The couple had been one of the African-American families who had benefited from long term employment at the Jewell Company. Both husband and wife had worked for years with Jesse, using their income to send Ben Jr. through medical school, second son Walter through law school and their younger daughters to receive teaching degrees. Calls and letters came from friends who had served on industry boards with Jesse. Former customers inquired about Jesse's health and wished him well, but as the span of years following his stroke moved off the calendar, the calls and inquiries lessened. As the slowing in Jesse's schedule began to become routine, it allowed time for one of the strangest occurrences to take place in Jesse Jewell's life.

After Jesse had begun his recovery, Pat notice a profound change in her father's personality. At first, she explained it to herself as a just a result of the stroke, but looking back she's convinced that the deep change was of a more profound initiative than what a stroke might have produced. First, he stopped drinking, and to the best of her knowledge, he never drank again. But the change didn't stop there. Once, when Bill Stowe came by to visit, he asked Jesse if there was anything he could get for him as he was leaving. "Yes", Jesse simply replied, "Bring me the Bible on tape."

Sometime later, he would request a Bible from Jack Prince. When Jack returned the next day, Jesse requested that Jack read to him from the new Bible. Jack had been close to Jesse since his and Pat's marriage, but he found it awkward at first to be reading the Bible to his father-in-law, but the habit of reading Scripture to Jesse would become a two to three times per week routine. Whether this interest in spiritual issues precipitated the meeting of Jesse and Odean McNeal, no one knows for sure. No one, family or friend, can recall how the two men would come to know each other, to the point of becoming close friends in what would be the autumn of each man's life.

Jack Prince thinks that perhaps Jesse called Odean after hearing one of his radio sermons.

McNeal was a Baptist minister who pastored several churches in the area during his career. He was of modest build and an almost shy demeanor until he stepped up to the podium to speak. His sermons were heard by spellbound congregations, convicting them of inconsistencies and bringing encouragement in the same message. His unwillingness to compromise on timeless truth had caused him to lose some pastorates and probably kept him from being offered some others.

He had grown up in the Chicopee Mill village just a few miles south of Gainesville. Tom Paris Jr. remembers Odean as one of the best athletes he ever saw play any sport. Tom, who was offered a football scholarship at the quarterback position, and who would letter four years at the University of Georgia, had a chance to see several great athletes with whom to compare Odean. One of those was a quarterback named Fran Tarkenton who was the reason Tom played a lot more defensive back than quarterback. But Odean would become known and respected, even by those who disagreed with him, as a man of uncompromising integrity while quietly championing the less advantageous children of God's Kingdom. One former pastor peer of Odean's was heard to say that Odean McNeal and his wife found a way to give more money to and help the poor more than some entire individual churches. How he might have accomplished this on the meager pastor salary of his day remains as much a mystery as to how he came to know Jesse.

The skeptic might suspect that Odean was after money, but Jack Prince knew better. In the mid to late sixties, Jesse's financial situation had become bleak. Jack recalls sitting at the breakfast table one morning with Pat and discussing her parent's financial predicament. A large envelope stuffed with J.D. Jewell Inc. stock certificates lay on the table between them. The stock was basically worthless.

Later that year, Jack and Pat would have to disguise a cash gift, as a repayment of a long ago loan from Jesse to start their home, to provide Anna Lou with Christmas shopping funds. The loan had never actually happened, but Anna Lou was convinced by Pat to take the money.

Pat recalls that when Odean would visit Jesse, the two of them would sit on the porch talking quietly and laughing a lot. She never listened in on their conversation. After Jack Prince had left his father-in-law's employment to make an unsuccessful run for the U.S. Congress, he had started his own poultry equipment business. Working for the new owners of the Jewell Company was something he had never considered, but he and Jesse had remained close.

On his way home one afternoon, he stopped at his in-laws house to check on Jesse. He found him sitting in his favorite chair watching TV. Jack caught something about the National Guard and some students being shot on the campus of Kent State. After taking a seat across from him, he asked Jesse if he would like to have the Bible read today. Jesse remained silent for a while and Jack was not sure he had heard him as the TV continued to play. Finally Jesse asked Jack to turn the TV off. His next statement caught Jack completely by surprise.

"I'm afraid to die," he solemnly told Jack, "I don't think I've been good enough to go to Heaven."

At first, Jack didn't know what to say, and he silently prayed for discernment before he responded. Jack started, "You don't have to be good enough to go to Heaven, and actually no one can get there by being good."

When Jack paused, Jesse said that Odean had been telling him the same thing, and it just didn't seem right, adding that it went against everything he thought he had been taught in his earlier church going days. And although he would like to believe it, he knew he had done a lot of wrong things in his life and couldn't see how he could deserve it.

Jack then reached over to the coffee table where Jesse's Bible was lying. Without saying another word he turned to Ephesians 2: 8-9 and slowly read the verses to Jesse.

"See," Jack explained, "no one can earn their way there, Boss. The only way to get a ticket is to accept it as being free."

Jack continued to read a few verses from Romans including 3: 10 and 3: 23. Without comment he read Romans 10: 9. Jesse seemed to be listening intently and before placing the Bible back on the coffee table, Jack finished with John 3:16.

The men sat quietly for a few minutes until Jesse reached over and retrieved the Bible. He seemed to be looking for something as he flipped through the pages and found an index card with some handwriting on it.

"Odean said that if I would pray this prayer and if I meant it I would go to Heaven for sure. Have you ever done this Jack?"

As Jack took the card he immediately recognized what was often referred to as the sinner's prayer. "Yeah Jesse, I've done this. You want me to pray it with you?" When Jesse acknowledged by nodding his head, the two men bowed their heads and began to pray together.

This float was part of the Annual Poultry Parade
which was held each year in Gainesville.

CHAPTER 12

AS THE RICH RULE OVER THE POOR, THE BORROWER IS
A SLAVE TO THE LENDER — SOLOMON

One of the presidents that Chairman Carl Chandler had hired to run the Jewell Company had decided to move the company offices into downtown on the fourth and fifth floors of the First Federal Savings and Loan building. The five story structure was a modern looking building boasting wide hallways and an impressive entrance leading to its one elevator. Company executive offices were located on the fifth floor while lesser management and accounting was on the fourth. Not long after the move, the landlord was approached about adding a second elevator. The Jewell company president did not think it seemed proper for top executives to be fraternizing and riding with other tenants and the staff on the floors below. With the landlord's approval, but with $100,000 of the Jewell Company's money, the second elevator was installed.

Skip Hope was usually the first one to arrive at the 311 Green Street offices. The newly paved parking lot surrounding the Southern Federal Building was already radiating heat from the June sun. As Skip turned the car radio off, he heard something about the break-in of some hotel by the name of Watergate in Washington. But his mind was not on the morning news; it was on the Company's annual report that he had helped to prepare.

The year was 1972 and lying before him on his desk, Skip had the annual reports for each of the previous ten years following the buyout of Jesse Jewell. Even though more product was being sold annually, the company had lost money every year. Rumors were beginning to be passed among customers and suppliers, and growers were being lost to other poultry plants almost weekly.

While the company president and top management were having a "two martini lunch" at the Country Club, Skip along with the folks in his department, determined that there was not enough cash to meet payroll. He reluctantly took the elevator to the fifth floor, which until recently, he rarely visited. Mr. Chandler was out, but his secretary promised to forward him the grim news as soon as possible.

For the remainder of the summer and into early fall, the company struggled to meet its obligations. Borrowing more money was no longer an option as most sources of credit had been depleted. Early in October, Carl Chandler called a meeting of all personnel in the fourth floor breakroom. He then calmly announced that the J.D. Jewell Company would be entering a Chapter 11 bankruptcy. He even sounded confident as he encouraged each one to keep working as the company would take this opportunity to reorganize and start a new day.

When the meeting was over, he called Skip aside and told him that he was the new company treasurer. Skip was not flattered, but he was loyal. As a young man he had inwardly hoped that the company would make it. A lot of people depended on that, starting with his friends in accounting and the customers and suppliers. But Skip knew that the people who would be hit the hardest with the potential closing were the plant people.

Later in the week, Skip was introduced to Robert Hicks. Mr. Hicks was an attorney from one of the large Atlanta law firms who had been assigned by the bankruptcy court as trustee. Although friendly, the trustee was all business. The official date of the bankruptcy was 20 October, 1972. On the 30th of October, after having reviewed company books with Skip during the previous week, Mr. Hicks asked Skip to summon Mr. Chandler down to the fourth floor. When Carl Chandler came into Skip's office, it appeared that he already knew what was going to happen. The conversation was short and to the point.

"This company can no longer afford you. Get your stuff and leave immediately" were the only words spoken by Mr. Hicks.

Carl Chandler never said a word and Skip never saw him again. One month later, the processing plant closed, putting hundreds of hourly workers, many who had been with the company for years, on the street looking for jobs.

Skip Hope would later team up with his old friend, Jan Cooley, and work for him until his retirement. At one point, during one of the interviews with Skip, he stopped talking and just grew quiet for a few moments. Then, as it seemed he had been collecting his thoughts he simply said," You know, on every October 20th since then, I remember that day. I think of Mr. Jewell. He really was a great man."

Debby Kroll had been accepted to graduate school at the University of Notre Dame but was struggling with when to start her studies. As the oldest of the Jewell grandchildren she had enjoyed a special bond with her grandfather. Now her grandfather was dying. The year was 1975 and the country was in a true recession as the housing and real estate market had been on downhill skids. There was no hurry to get to South Bend even if her acceptance might be jeopardized. She decided that it would not make any difference; if her grandfather was passing away, she would be here for him and her mother.

Approximately one year after the bankruptcy, Jesse's health had started to decline. Whether the demise of his old company had anything to do with his physical state is not known, but Pat remembers that her dad had little to say about the closing or the people involved. Back in 1964, a banquet honoring his accomplishments had been held at the

Chattahoochee Country Club. The guest list was a who's who of poultry industry leaders along with state and local dignitaries. For several years Jesse had attempted to stay in touch with the people at the Plant by going to lunch with Skip Hope and Jan Cooley. Cooley had been fired as quality control manager for refusing to release some undercooked precooked product. Although it would be another two decades before Cooley's own poultry empire would come to fruition, Jesse must have begun to realize that with the departure of men like Cooley, Haskell Stratton and Jack Prince, that the handwriting was on the wall. He had no control in the company's closing, and knew that everyone who had any knowledge of what had happened did not hold him responsible. But his name had remained on the marquee and it was his customers and employees who had suffered.

During the last few years of his life, he didn't get out much and the visits by old friends like Howard Fuller and Odean McNeal were his only contacts outside of family. Although the diagnoses and treatment of stroke victims was advancing, twenty five years later Jesse would have probably been treated for what was most likely a series of small strokes that had left him physically and mentally incapacitated.

The concept of in home hospice was not yet practiced and for the last several months of 1974, Jesse was in and out of the hospital. In early January, Janet arrived from Los Angeles to see her father for what would be the last time. He could not talk nor did he seem to recognize her. With her schedule requiring her to return, she left when it appeared that Jesse had rebounded a little, at least physically. No longer than she had returned home than Pat called to report that he had taken a turn for the worse and the doctors had told the family that his death was imminent.

Barbara arrived from Arizona in Gainesville before Janet and joined the rest of the family at the hospital. Debby had been beside her grandfather's bed for most of the day. She talked calmly with him as she kept his mouth moist with small spoons of crushed ice. Barbara took a seat beside Debby and took her dad's hand. Jesse had not spoken or really responded to anyone for the past several days. Barbara, who was not known to be a religious person, reached over to a night stand and retrieved a Gideon Bible from the top drawer. At first Debby was not sure of what her aunt was about to do. The aunt and niece were considered to be kindred spirits and Debby, having grown up close to her aunt, knew her not to be one inclined to call on Scripture. As she sat there somewhat surprised, Barbara asked her father if he would like for her to read the Bible to him. Debby was amazed at what happened next. Jesse began to blink his eyes affirmatively and then Barbara found the 23rd Psalm and began to read. As she read, large tears rolled down Jesse's cheeks. Janet recalls vividly the tears and the look of contentment that came over his face. When Barbara finished reading, Jesse smiled, and then took a deep breath. It would be his last.

Even though he had arrived early, Skip Hope sat almost in the back of the sanctuary of the First Baptist Church on Green Street, the same street that Jesse had taken hundreds of times over the years on his way to build a company and an industry. All seats were taken and Skip heard later that many more waited outside unable to hear any of the eulogies. Skip didn't hear them either because his mind went back to those days that he had carried Jesse Jewell to lunch. He knew that he was privileged to have had the honor of spending some time with the man that had started the industry that he and thousands more would find a livelihood. He also knew that he was witnessing a defining moment for that industry. Be it good or bad, the future would not be the same, because an era had just come to an end.

EPILOGUE

As of this writing, the poultry industry worldwide produces millions of pounds of chicken. Americans today eat more chicken than beef and pork combined. Would there have been a poultry industry without Jesse Dickson Jewell? Would there be an automobile industry without Henry Ford? The answer is yes to both questions. But entrepreneurial giants like Jewell and Ford gave their respective industries a significant jump start with their God given gifts of ingenuity and energy. Like Ford, Jewell's work ethic was eclipsed only by his gift for innovatively thinking outside the box.

Ben Carter recalled, "Every day he had a new idea on how to make more money."

Yet, from other interviews with the men and women who worked with him or did business with Jesse Jewell, greed was not a motivating factor in his quest for growth and expansion. He was described by several of his contemporaries as "being generous to a fault". Several of his high ranking managers were appalled by his willingness to share existing methods and future ideas with potential or actual competitors.

To Jewell, the fun and fulfillment was in the trip, not getting to the destination. Once a project was up and running, or written off as a failure, he actually became bored with it and left its day to day operations, in the case of failure the picking up the pieces, delegated to others.

Myrtle Figueras, the former councilwoman and mayor of Gainesville, Georgia spoke these words at the dedication of the State of Georgia, brass historical marker shown below:

"Friends, family and citizens, what a fitting tribute we share here today, as we recognize such a great giant who has been labeled the poultry pioneer on his headstone. Gainesville's status all over the world is one that each of us enjoys because of the dressing plants, the hatcheries, the feed mills, the rendering plants, the poultry science companies, the marketing and advertising and other affiliated business which serve to boost the quality of life of the poultry capital of the world."

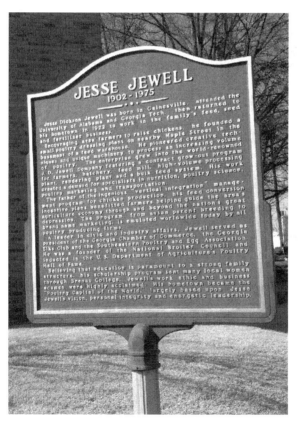

State of Georgia Historical Marker on Jesse Jewell Parkway

When Jesse Jewell recognized potential in a young man or woman, he would hire them immediately and worry about a place and job description later.

Yet, as Bob Sealey recalls, "He put his pants on each morning just like all the rest of us."

And human he was in more ways than one. In business, he made some poor choices, the Lincoln-Mercury dealership acquisition being one glaring example, but there were others. However, most recalled that it didn't seem to get him down or despondent. Rarely did he complain over "spilled milk." He seemed to always have the self-confidence to know that with hard work, he could recover from any goof. He was not remembered by anyone that this author interviewed as being high handed or arrogant, although his position and accomplishments would have made many others of us to become so. He rarely fired anyone, but when he did it was swift and without apology.

Most of his employees, from the line workers to management, found him to be accessible. His generosity to them at times, like the annual Christmas party, was rare in American business. Power and prestige did not seem to have great appeal to Jesse Jewell. Although he served as president or chairman of several of the industry and civic organizations, simply stated, the general consensus was, that he enjoyed "doing business" and doing a lot of it.

In personal and family relations, Jewell was made of flesh and bone. Jack Prince and I spent many hours over a cup of coffee discussing the human side of Jesse Jewell. A strong friendship (at least I'd like to think) developed between Jack and me as I picked his brain about the life of his father-in-law. Jack is a business person of considerable accomplishments in the poultry industry as well. But, I came to respect him for his character and spirit.

On one occasion as we discussed Mr. Jewell's personal life, it occurred to me that Jesse Jewell could have some skeletons in his closet. I mentioned this to Jack and assured him I was not interested in uncovering some hidden scandal and taking tabloid approach to this writing. Jack assured me that Jesse Jewell was indeed human and was not perfect. But, to the best of his knowledge, he could never recall an incident of moral failure or impropriety. If there was, he was not consistent in the behavior for it to become an open way of life. Jack's eyes misted even as he added that he admired Jesse Jewell more than any other man he has ever known.

During a dinner one evening, again on the Gainesville Square, at Two Dog Café, my wife and I sat and listened as Jack's wife, Pat, the oldest of three Jewell's daughters, remember her father. Being the oldest, and in her formative years, correspondingly with her father's busiest days of building the business, Pat recalls a loving, but strict Dad who took his role as provider and defender very seriously. Even though not considered affluent at the time, she was taught by example not to look down on other children who came from families of less advantage. Pat would enter and graduate from UNC. Her dad set high expectations for her, but just as he did with his employees, he gave her great latitude in accomplishing her task.

During one of our last coffee sessions before the publishing of this book, I asked Jack if Jesse Jewell was a religious man. He explained to me that the Jewell family attended a local church regularly and that Jesse approached church activities as he did secular community and business endeavors. Although not with hypocrisy, church was, as best Jack could determine, just another good cause that Jewell felt obliged to contribute.

Then after some pause and reflection, Jack recalled some last conversations the two had. Mr. Jewell began to discuss some of the theological issues and even asked Jack to regularly read some scripture passages. Jack discovered that this many who had accomplished so much still had an empty hole and unfilled void in his life. Jack, who is an evangelical Christian began to explain the concept of grace to him. And, that although he had earned every accomplishment that he had achieved in life, according to New Testament theology, he could not earn his way into eternity with God. And that Jesus Christ was who He claimed to be and not just a historical figure or mythical hero.

Then during one conversation, Jack read a series of verses from the book Romans, referred to in Christian circles as the "Roman Road". When he finished, Mr. Jewell bowed his head. The man who had built and accumulated a business and fortune, who had started an industry, and whose name is on street signs of major thoroughfare in the city where he lived and died, whispered a prayer and humbly accepted something that he did not deserve or earn. Perhaps this will be his longest lasting legacy of all.

Family portrait of Jesse and Anna Lou Jewell with their daughters:
(left to right) Patricia, Janet, Barbara

About the Author

Homer Myers spent his childhood on his grandparents two mule farm. Around age 8 or 9 he actually plowed a mule named Kate, even though she was on automatic pilot. He attended Hall County public schools and entered North Georgia College in fall of 1969. Graduating with a 2.0000 GPA, he entered the U.S Army as a 2nd Lt., (a military professor at NGC told him upon his commissioning that he was, "bullet stopping material" and guaranteed him a place in the Infantry). His real education came from working with a brick mason for 8 summers through High School and college. After leaving the Army his plan was to continue in the construction business. But 1974 was the peak of a severe real estate recession and construction had come to a standstill. Myers entered the life insurance business in 1974 until he could find something better to do and as of today, 44 years later, he still hasn't found anything.

His wife Renee has remained married to him for over 45-years now-God bless her. She is a retired public school teacher. Their two sons have provided one grandchild each which has kept them in the will. Myers claims to be the favorite grand parent of his bossy grand-daughter and younger grandson.

Even having written three books, he has had no real success as a writer although he claims to have made enough money on them to buy a chain saw.